Sea Scale

By the same author:

and dug my fingers in the sand (2000)
Misplaced Heart (2003)
Uncommon Light (2007)
Collusion (2012)
Have Been and Are (2016)

Sea Scale
New & Selected Poems

Brook Emery

PUNCHER & WATTMANN

© Brook Emery 2022

This book is copyright. Apart from any fair dealing for the purposes of study and research, criticism, review or as otherwise permitted under the Copyright Act, no part may be reproduced by any process without written permission. Inquiries should be made to the publisher.

First published in 2022
Published by Puncher and Wattmann
PO Box 279
Waratah NSW 2298

http://www.puncherandwattmann.com
puncherandwattmann@bigpond.com

A catalogue entry for this book is available from the National Library of Australia.

ISBN 9781925780090

Cover design by Miranda Douglas

Cover image by Helena Lewerenz

Printed by Lightning Source International

This project has been assisted by the Australian Government through the Australia Council, its arts funding and advisory body.

for M'Lady Zadie

Contents

Sea Scale : New Poems

Self Portrait : Provisional Sketch	15
Devote Less Time	23
Rendezvous	24
Pickpocket	26
The Heart of the Matter	27
Meditating	28
as if / the moth	29
As Light Seeps In	32
Implicated Witness	33
The Stars at Night	34
In the Art Gallery	35
Tree Roots, Bellingen	36
Undiminished	41
Contra Lorca	42
A Shaft of Sunlight	44
Joe Palooka	45
Voltage Across a Membrane	46
The Eremite in his Cave	52
Between Time	53
The Traveller Reminisces	54
My Bald Head	56
Letter to Tristram Shandy, Gentleman	57
Big-Time Wrestling	58
Culture	60
The Dandelion's Puffball	61
On or About December 1910	62
Velcro	64
Half the Sins	65

Posthumous Existence	66
The Kid on the Billycart	68
Self Portrait : Sea Scale	69

and dug my fingers in the sand (2000)

and dug my fingers in the sand	81
Physical	85
Song of Songs	86
Cowboys	87
My Father's Eyes	88
Shellac	90
With My Father-in-law	92
Crossing the Border	96
Infidelity	97
Improvising with Flaubert	98
Underfoot	104
Letter to a Live Poet	105
any and all means	107
The Distance and the Heat	109
At a Slight Angle	110
Approaching the Edge	111

Misplaced Heart (2003)

The mind is a small bird hovering	119
Sunday	120
A Raven Before the Dove	121
Letter While Flying	124
The mind is a tightrope walker balanced	126
Let it go (hold on to)	127

We do only be drowned now and again	132
The mind is a body breathing in unconsciously	138
The mind is a kind of theatre and we	139
Aubade and Evensong : New Year 2003	140
Prequel : Sequel	142
Commentary : Two Days	143
The mind is the surface of a pond expanding	145
For a Child	146
For My Brother and Sister	147
And asked her how she was	148
Final Belief	150
The mind is a misplaced heart lopsidedly	152
Postscript : Like Picasso	153

Uncommon Light (2007)

Spring	157
Very Like a Whale	158
Morning : Thinking of You	161
Finches Perhaps	162
Monster	163
Sunday : (Everything can be) transformed	165
That Beat Against the Cage	168
'Am I really the person who bears my name?'	172
Monster	175
Against Immortality	177
Tourism : what the I sees	178
Uncommon Light	181
Thirty-six Views of Bondi Beach	186
Monster	192
Narcissus : self portrait with sea	194
Half-glimpsed through water	196

This Disenchanted World	197
Monster	199
Spring is Still Spring (Summer)	200

Collusion (2012)

Dear K, it's light that makes the river flow	203
After the lassitudes of blue	204
It's almost spring in our neglected hemisphere	207
In the hour or so before night's certain fall	208
Waking at night silence has the colour	209
All morning it's been difficult to settle	211
A low pressure cell is tracking up the coast	213
I remember very little	214
I want to say the word 'adrift'	216
You know the way a snatch of song	218
I can eclipse you with a wink	220
Contested ground, this strange persistent beauty	221
It appears we are machines to manufacture words	224
In the background there is the music	225
Gloom off to the west	226
I walk among the dead	228
Autumn warmth is draining from the day	229
I almost understand this resonance	230
Rain as it is only brighter	232

Have Been and Are (2016)

And the word 'environment'	235
Brain doesn't improvise	241
We are lashed to our body	242

The poet is a centipede	243
Body is but a striving	244
At the end of the mind	245
To get the better of words	246
The rain falls down	247
The most important experience of being	248
Everything waste	250
Only keep still, wait, and hear	253
Echo, repetition, statement	255
The brown current	257
A preposterous hodgepodge	265
What were they then	267
The lightness, the non-mass of it	268
There on the shore	272
A steady delete	273
Drive, he sd	274
I should be rolling down the skyway	275
Stately, plump Buck Mulligan	276
You want ghosts	277
A spring day like this	281
Endless forms most beautiful and wonderful	283
Broken / Beautiful	290

Sea Scale : New Poems

Listen: a fourworded wave speech: seesoo, hrss, rsseeiss, ooos. Vehement breath of waters ...

James Joyce, *Ulysses*

Self Portrait : Provisional Sketch

How then shall we proceed? Word by word, fearlessly,
cautiously, line by line, one foot after another, again
and then again, seduced by the pull of a sentence
(as Marianne Moore would have it) into near and far,
where an umbrella and a sewing machine
circle uneasily on a dissecting table: implausible,
but interesting none-the-less. I write now
what I couldn't write before or after, the inner
out of oneself, out in the world, write myself
as other in the 'I', doubling, tripling,
twisting in and out of shape. Reason is all we have,
reason lets go, is not near enough. Consider the body
and its out-of-body, the between where unknown waits.
I make my memories now, the gut a second brain,
skin a free-trade zone where words are coins.

'Lugubrious,' there's a word to conjure with,
what a mournful mouthful, which brings to mind
'lucubrate,' lubricious,' 'luscious,' but this
could go on forever: pellucid, lucid, limpid,
even *Lumen Scientiae* that long-forgotten motto
of my old school where we studied Latin, French
and German, conjugated, parsed, analysed, and made sure
subject and verb were always in agreement. Once
we reduced Miss Dan to tears. Years later
I directed tourists to Père Lachaise Cemetery
in a Deutscher-Franglish mishmash which quite possibly
left them lost for decades. The mind moves of its own accord,
sound and sense not consistently harmonious,

and I must dwell amid the tumult of the dictionary
(Is that Pasternak? This second-hand thinking
has to stop!). 'Bamboozle', now that's a word!
What might be its derivation, who might have
coined it? Should I look it up or let it be its own
hypnotic, almost onomatopoeic self? 'Hornswoggle',
boondoggle, befuddle, lollapalooza.

Nothing is without precedent, not a word,
not a thought, not the Big Bang or even DNA.
In the beginning so much was promised of the word
yet, in the trip from mouth to ear, mind to page
and back again, so much remains splattered
against the dark wall of a cave, a sentence
becoming letter by letter or plucked complete
from the outer reaches of the planet, the buried recesses
of the brain: a superfluity of meaning,
a lack of sufficient meaning. 'Hardwired', some say, forgetting
the word itself is malleable, in fact a metaphor
from a recently faded age. Is metaphor inimical to thinking
or essential? Ask Hobbes, ask Vico, don't ask me!
My littlest granddaughter, almost one, waves her hand
like Queen Elizabeth and almost says, 'bye bye',
She recognises 'nose' and 'hands on head',
makes herself understood in grunts and squawks
and gestures. Her cousin Buster, at eighteen months,
pronounced his first full sentence, 'Birds all gone',
when rosellas feeding from his outstretched arms
suddenly took flight. An infant, by derivation,
is a child who has not yet learnt to speak. Soon each of them
will have so much more to say than me.

My shadow stalks me or I it, shadow mind
shadowed brain, now behind, now beside,
losing its way in thought: Could I be body?
Am I myself? What do I have to say?
Pinned foot to foot I print my shadow
on the footpath: grey on grey, it's never
far away. Mirrored buildings fashion a second
more glistening me. I wave, I skip, I jump,
pull a funny face, and my reflection
doesn't hesitate to ape me. Gorilla, it says,
seahorse, it says, insect, elephant, frog, dolphin, bat,
swarm of bees, a carousel of painted words.
You're not so very special, no matter what you think.
I'm talking to you, Sunny Jim, and to my buried self,
trying to unearth what lies beneath time,
where the mind might live, where words like flim-flam,
gewgaw and folderol might usefully reside.
Are we not Schrödinger's shadow cat, asleep and dreaming,
bright-eyed and awake, coherently alive and dead?
I am seen so I must exist. I am heard so I must be.
'What is life?' Schrödinger asked, but didn't answer.

Today, we huddle inside, wish for air conditioning,
wish for fans, complain of February's heat
as though it wasn't always so, and suddenly
it feels like 1959 again: the Bondi tram
is running on time, and the one down the cutting
to Bronte Beach; milkshakes are malted
and come in metal cups; milk is delivered to our door

by horse and cart, bread too: and the Southerly Buster
— the leading edge of memory — is on its way.
In our boys' school canes fall on proffered hands,
fights erupt in the playground, and star knives
are flung across the classroom during the Shintaro craze.
In Science, Sludge Solomon flicks a match
into a Bunsen Burner and sets alight my eyebrows.
We write parodies of Eliot instead of essays,
skip classes and go swimming at Parsley Bay.
We were ratbags, billiard balls of energy
cannoning off each other in a
hang-the-consequences frenzy, our reflective lives
a very private matter. Morning tea was a finger bun,
lunch a pie. I'd forgotten this. It doesn't signify.
What I'm worrying about here, Archie Ammons
mulled over before me in the archly titled 'garbage'.
There he wrote that language is important
but is not the world: 'grooming does for baboons
most of what words do for us' (and, I confess,
I've done violence to his lineation). Clouds are massing now,
the sky is darker, the wind is getting up, and suddenly
a thunderbolt seems to split the house asunder.
The baby's eyes are wide, but there's no evidence of tears.
The world outside the self, impinging, imposing.
Nothing personal you understand (*how admirable —
a man who sees lightning / and not satori*).

I interrogate the past for clues, incidents, coincidence,
though correlation, I know, may not be cause.
You cannot 'be' without before, can't remember
or forget without a past, even what has been forgone.

How much will I retain of even this, how explain it all
in words? I started but never finished *À La Recherche
du Temps Perdu*: now I'll never have the time.
Words are not thoughts or things, though the literal
may dress in a figure's lineaments (or *vice versa*),
and boundaries are not clear. *What is your substance,
whereof are you made, that millions of strange shadows
on you tend?* Those are words. That's genius. For the rest of us
the shabby counterfeit, the plod, plod, plod
to 'thingummyjig' or 'thingummybob',
to yabber-yabber, bunkum and balderdash. Pierre-Simon
marquis de Laplace postulated an intellect so vast
'no things would be uncertain, and the future,
just like the past, would be present before its eyes.'
Is this a curse, worse by far than total recall?
We see the bits we want to see, hear the words
we have heard so many times before, respond
as we are expected to react, *vide:* the placebo effect,
the nocebo effect. A green sun sets,
a black sun rises. O, to amass incontrovertible words,
to testify fully and truthfully, without guile or indecision,
though the past be swimming and full of smoke.

Can the mind be simultaneously consistent and complete?
The answer may have passed this way, may be hiding
in the words, erased and re-worked, erased again,
the derivative masquerading as original,
perpetually pitoning up the same sheer mountain face,
perpetually slippery-sliding down again, confounded
by the impulses of the heart, the temptations of the eye,
the doublespeak of distinctions with very little difference.

Is it possible to be a body without a mind,
or a mind without a body? Come, you Greeks,
come Descartes, to my assistance! Is it
matter within mind, mind within matter,
or something markedly different? The mind as literally
an analytical engine, nothing more, nothing less –
it does not compute. And where might 'Fancy' fit,
that archaic supposition? Might it bridge the gulf
between the atolls of 'I feel' and the promontory
'I think'? Or is Fancy just another observed firing
in an isolated landscape of the brain? *To keep language alive,
to keep alive the idea of seriousness,*
that's the job of literature, Susan Sontag declared.

I'm harvesting motes and mites and mights
from the past, re-telling an interrupted story to myself,
grubbing for words which make thinking come alive,
words to answer the question, 'What was it like?'
But why, when it's the present which has passed me by:
a pale male, still hale, a little stale; not unhappy, just befuddled
and bemused. We used to eat Chiko Rolls, Sargents Pies,
Pluto Pups, Polly Waffles, Rainbow Balls, chop and three veg;
now I hear earnest talk of spirulina, whey powder,
acai bowls, pepitas, kale, quinoa, goji berries, oxygen enhanced
bottled water, and god knows what else: holistic wellness,
mindfulness, celestial massage. I know McDonalds
and Kentucky Fried purvey fat but I'm persuaded
the present may be healthier than the past and,
although I'm sounding a little lugubrious, curmudgeonly even,
there's nothing that I'm pining for or need. I do wonder though
where I might fit in. I don't scroll or troll or trawl,

I don't podcast, blog, or follow anyone on Twitter,
I don't do Instagram, Facebook, Tinder, or bespoke history
on Ancestry.com. Hashtag, I admit, 'haplessandhelpless'
and I'm at a loss to know what LOL, LMK, OMG, WTF
or those self-spawning emojis might conceivably mean.
I'm an analogue fish flummoxed in a digital sea.
Too much mumbo-jumbo, too much piffle,
not enough pith. I have no brand, no virtual footprint,
ipso facto there's no proof I exist, or ever have.

I seem to have gone a bit skew-whiff
in the aforesaid. Despite my intention, this poem has become lament,
a debased form trailing threads of self-indulgence
and nostalgia. Would it were a proper threnody, an elegy,
or prophecy, something with gravitas, oomph. It is, I know,
'a tissue of quotations' (thank you, Roland Barthes)
but what can one do when just about everything
has been thought and said. At least this poem is not a cento
where ALL the lines belong to someone else; and
it's not plagiarised — all citations are attributed,
and the allusions are easy to spot. Flaubert
posed the question, 'Is it splendid or stupid
to take life seriously?', and despaired he stood poised
above the matching perils of lyricism and vulgarity.
Into which chasm have I fallen? May I be redeemed?
In pre-dawn light I walk past weathered headstones
refiguring the hillside and read their graven testaments —
'weep not for me', 'thy will be done'.
The sun rises, the crescent moon lingers in the sky,
Venus, the morning star, watches over it all
like a guardian angel. I think of my granddaughter,

M'Lady Zadie, who is probably just waking up,
and of the surf which thoughtlessly embraces me,
flings me in the air and tumbles me under the foam,
a body against and through the bodily (as someone wrote).
What help is a dictionary to describe such plenitude?
This is a moment to savour, but here, though I luxuriate,
I cannot dillydally. Invisibly we are drawn back to our thinking selves,
to the perennial questions we puzzle again and again,
to the provisional answers which beg to be revised,
to the devalued currency of our words. Allow me a last quotation:
The poem is the possibility of happiness (Baudelaire).

Devote less time, O Poet,
staring into the mirror:
you can't write your own reviews.

Rendezvous

Even standing still it's flickering this way and that,
the mind, that dematerialised, invisible thing,
swaying like a ship's light in a storm,
picking out memories, slights, landmarks
which may not exist at all, plotting a future
which may never come. I hear it talking secretively,

flipping from labyrinth to waterfall to field of wheat,
from scorpion to red-bellied black to tangled thicket
and fast flowing stream already threatening
to break its banks: feather, wing, teetering branch,
a cavity beneath a hollow log, teeming insect life.
The mind, that uncertain interlinear thing

weaving between and through the clouds,
rumbling thunder, sheet lightning, and the after-image
which effloresces behind closed lids:
sun shower, followed by deluge, drizzle,
footprints in wet grass, the dissolving life of mud,
the tramp who leaves never/always to return.

The mind, that imagined, un-located thing,
ringing on and off like an unanswered phone –
please leave a message – the unconnected
farrago of clicks and tones, the breathy pause,
exhalations and exasperations, a night sky
constellation of comets and dying stars.

The mind, a late night stop on a country road,
the dashboard lights turned low, the radio
a fuzz of static, the engine idling and revving
spasmodically; on the passenger seat an empty wallet,
an envelope, a child's drawing of a gun; the misted windows
framing a time and place for the rendezvous.

Pickpocket

You wake up one morning and suddenly ...

your children are middle-aged. And the toddler next door
is an elegant young lady in an evening gown
on her way to sing soprano in the Opera House choir ...

your children's children are all in school
learning to calculate and compromise. But the blonde,
nut-brown little girl running across the lawn
with a feather clutched in her hand is unchanged
though she's more than forty now. How does this happen?

How did it happen that at this particular moment
yesterday and today traded places or occupied,
temporarily, the same space – a big screen, split-screen experience?
Memory, perforce, is always a matter of then and now,
and mostly beyond our control. It contrives
to catch us off-guard, pick time past
from our empty pockets or put it back again.
Nothing mysterious here, other than a dawning realisation:

that the obvious can still surprise is, in itself, a surprise.

The Heart of the Matter

I'm walking the edge of sandstone cliffs
beside the cemetery, looking out to sea or down
where waves lap against the sloping shelf
and slip between broken slabs which have fallen
who knows how long ago. Sometimes, more excitingly,
I'll watch swells take shape way out to sea, line up, lift,
and gather speed and size before exploding
against the rocks with a resounding thump.

They hurl themselves skywards, claw at crevice
and crack, drain back and mingle with the next wave
battering this steep margin: a blurred dividing line
where unknowing is thrust against hard-edged certainty,
where the scientific truth that matter is movement –
restless, oscillating particles tensely bound –
is almost imaginable though it is hard
to think beyond the seen, the commonsense:
Newton's physics are enough to get us to the moon;
it's another leap to fly Einstein's inter-stellar time.

To be awake, truly awake, to the scale of things
is a type of exile, though it is relative not absolute.

We live on the fringe, not at the heart of matter.

Meditating
on a cliff's rim
imperils equilibrium

as if / the moth
might have a clue for me

(David Brooks, 'A Call from Mandelstam')

Insects swarm in wing-wrought clouds,
assume fantastic shapes — dragons, salamanders,
serpents, chimera resolving and dissolving
as I sweep my head from yesterday
into tomorrow. Here's time, here's chance,
the wilful self-deception which turns 'I see'
into 'I think' and no, please no,
into I believe ...

                  ... we stumble through the Anthropocene,
stub toes, scratch cheeks, fall exhausted
to our knees, fear with its fingers at our throats.
Sightless and wingless birds plunge from the clouds,
drones hover and sweep like metallic dragonflies,
a sunken moon, a star, a comet, the criss-cross tracery
of a wintering tree, all stare back at us
from the blackened surface of a lake
and it all makes sense, it all
seems different — what was once familiar
hard against the unfamiliar ...

                ... Gods imaginable and unimaginable
drift down, nest in trees, perch on fence posts,
recline on balconies. Some have names like Donald,
Joseph, L-, others are more exotic. Some think thousands,
some billions, others can't conceive a beginning
or an end, while others, stern gods, punishing gods,
divine the death of time. They dress outlandishly,

some in feathers, some in silk, some
with armour-plating on their breasts. One
looks like a bumblebee, one looks like a man.
I should talk to them. There's nothing
I can think to say ...

                 ... Safely in the bygone, Marinetti
drives his flash car through the countryside
burbling incoherently about speed, energy,
'the sun's red sword,' 'the slap and the punching fist.'
Forward. Onward. His roadster hurtles into a muddy ditch.
Marinetti walks away unscathed yet fails to realise
the future calls him history. Osip Mandelstam
mocks Stalin for his cockroach moustache, is exiled,
released, re-arrested, and dies shivering in a transit camp:
there is no need for words. In America, Jim Harrison
walks his dogs beside the flooded river. With his remaining,
just-about-good eye he looks to the mountain ranges
which surround him. On the one called Crazies
he imagines perhaps a deer, perhaps a grizzly bear,
shrugs, turns back towards the shack where he'll write
and sweat the sleepless night *trying to make music and reason
out of the ocean of life ...*

                 ...We are orphans
pleading for time, arriving and departing,
taking leave of our sentences; the past
alive and disguised, the dead and soon dead
jostling for places, protesting their precedence.
Someone's been reading Joel, someone Acts,
someone the Book of Revelation. They wait.
They watch. They can't wait another minute.
They're listening for a peal of thunder, for a trumpet

blasting from the clouds. I think of laughter,
I think of scorn. I think what if they could be right,
in ways that should be wrong. Our minds won't do
what our minds ought to do ...

                        ... The night
falls over my neighbour's house like a shroud.
From somewhere I hear the word 'lickety-split'
and want to respond but all I can think to say
is 'nescience'. I imagine drops of water, drizzle, rain,
and seeping through the cracked and crazy paving
of the earth, a forgotten subterranean stream.
Green shoots sprout. Frogs and walking fish appear,
crickets begin their whirring, cicadas
who have spent years beneath the dirt
start to sing. Flies zigzag and buzz and spiders
lay out their intricate webs in expectation.
Then moths, insistent outside my windowpane,
fluttering there, brushing against the glass,
reluctant to concede the light is beyond their reach,
fine dust flickering in the restless beat of their wings.

As Light Seeps In

You wake in that sweet moment between night and day …

and nothing is quite the same. Yes, light seeps quietly in
as it usually does, and there, now, the first birds
are calling up the sun …

Let us sing you now, they carol, and as the notes rise
you know the world without you must be infinite …

All the stars, all the raindrops, all grains of sand,
all numberless, all invitations to calculate.
Matter to be measured against so that you are found wanting,
unable to see into the heart which is hidden in plain sight …

This is knowing what you are unable to see, it is
reason's opposite, the memory of a taste but not the taste,
it is listening to silence, to the song about
how people turn into other things.

It is standing on the platform alone as night creeps in …

on either side trains pull into the accumulating dark,
passengers staring ahead in yellow carriage light.

Implicated Witness

You wake in a hotel bed in a distant city ...

Light through venetian blinds falls across your body in slats.

The bedclothes are undisturbed as though last night
you had been laid out on top of the eiderdown
like a corps prepared for viewing. You lie here for some time
empty of thought about thoughts, even this one ...

You have no consciousness of rising but find yourself outside.

The air is crisp, so crisp it cracks against your eyelids
and everything is sharply defined — hard-edged buildings,
the curve of the bridge, glints of light on the river
as it rushes by. The blue sky is unrelenting,
yet everything is ambiguous, threatening ...

You are standing on a corner which cannot be recognised.
The streets are empty, space without presence.
Perhaps, unwittingly, you have been spliced into someone else's life ...

Where, after all, does the mind stop and the world begin?

You can't attest to what you see, your witness is not verified
or verifiable, you are implicated, you are not sure how,
and thinking cannot extricate you. Everything says, 'succumb.'

Rain begins to fall, sheer and clean. Almost invisibly
it strikes your upturned face. You can't be sure if this is the future
or the past, or something else as yet unnamed ...

You think it might be 'now'. It cannot last much longer.

The stars at night
are measuring time:
set your clock to 'distant'

In the Art Gallery

It's late autumn, the maple leaves
are scudding across the footpath, collecting in drifts
at the base of walls, clumping in ponds, and the children

are kicking up russet flurries in the park. On walking sticks
two elderly ladies are picking their way gingerly
against an unrelenting sun and the body's pesky limitations.

My friend is at work. I imagine her at her desk,
at her computer screen, answering the telephone
in pursuit of time which eludes her now and

will continue to elude her though she is aware that,
outside, morning has ceded to afternoon and soon
she will turn out the lights and walk home.

In the art gallery impressionist landscapes dream of light,
of change and changelessness, the complications
of frailty and strength in conjoined measures.

'Life goes on, things will change,' people say. But right now
there is a grief which annihilates time, which,
unbidden, has bound her in its corded arms. Grief speaks

of the mind's insufficiency, of the absence
of the body's body – the struggle to inhabit a space
that was once so familiar as to go unnoticed.

Of the horror of forever. The eye is unable
to see what the eye is seeing. Beauty is still beauty,
the future is still the future. But, oh, they are cruel.

Tree Roots, Bellingen: July-August, 2020

What are the roots that clutch, what branches grow
T.S. Eliot, *The Waste Land,* 'The Burial of the Dead'

A light frost sprinkles the yard and fog
makes willing prisoners of the trees.
Whip-birds split the air with their crisp whistle and crack.

Lorrikets zip, flash and squabble across the grass
and kookaburras, having sung their parts,
watch silently. Missy, the silvered cat,

lies curled inside the door like a ball of wool.
The lumpy and folded hills of the Great Dividing Range
thrust an unyielding purple into the just-blue sky.

This is prologue. Prefigurement. The moment which will change.

Red cedar was long-ago hacked from the valleys
of the Northern Rivers and carted to the sea. Now camphor laurels,
seeds widely scattered by cockatoos, currawongs,
magpies, firebirds, orioles and honeyeaters, out-compete
the native trees. Shallow, spreading roots weaken river banks.

Soon chainsaws will breach the headwaters of the Kalang,
timber jinkers bumping and barrelling along narrow,
winding roads through sleepy towns. The area is rich
and wet. In summer you can watch grass grow.

In rainforest areas, high leaves glisten in the sun,
the deeper you go the colder, darker it becomes.
Madeira vine, thick and vigorous, winds around
any available tree in a strangling embrace.
Lantana clumps in dense, thorny thickets.

The tributaries of the Kalang and Bellinger Rivers
saunter through the bush. Sometimes they trickle,
stranding pebbly graveyards mid-stream. With rain,
they surge beyond their banks, deposit debris
in the high limbs of trees, snarl fences,
flood bridges, bring down sally wattles, and rush sand,
mud, broken branches, weed, whole trees to the sea.

One Christmas, where the river washed across a sunken log,
we built a gleaming citadel above a tiny cataract.
Children sought out stones, hefted, balanced and positioned them,
argued architecture, engineering and aesthetics. Flat stones
were highly prized for beauty and stability. We fashioned towers,
ramparts, moats, courtyards, keeps, pools and dungeons.
Fortress and pleasure paradise, both. We foretold
a history, predicted it would withstand the ages.

Another year, the river rose at night. Suddenly
water was sloshing round the tents, the kayaks
were straining at their restraints, the swimming hole
was a foaming torrent and already
camp chairs, eskies, toothpaste, shoes had washed away.
By fumbled torchlight and tangled shouts,
in laughter and in terror, by confusion and good luck,
mattresses and tents, sleeping bags and clothes,

were dragged to higher ground and three generations
of sodden bodies slept, snored, snuffled and twitched
in their dreams on the carpeted lounge room floor.

Missy springs to the table, to the chair, to the lounge,
to my lap, leans in, nuzzles, and wordlessly
intimates a stroking would be acceptable.

She licks my fingers, purrs, stretches, and rolls over
to suggest it's time to have her tummy tickled.

Without warning, her claws drag across my wrist,
draw blood. She looks me in the eye, hops down, arches
and slinks away like an offended minor celebrity
at a fashion show: 'That's enough.

'A scratch for your trouble. There might be
a bird or a mouse to catch, a patch of late sun
to lie in. You can't expect me to admit ingratitude.
Don't think I'm oblivious to what's going on.'

The world presses in too hard. Contagion
locks us from our stadia and cafes.
We argue over masks and toilet paper, forget
the Aztecs, Mayans, Incas, the colonial trade
in measles, smallpox, mumps, chains and slaves.
Intractable, interminable, the present wars
fill TV screens and the Thirty Years War,
The Hundred Years War, the Frontier Wars, the Crusades,

the Holy Inquisition are all unread in history books.
One president bombs and gasses his people into rubble,
another declares himself king for life, another
is cruel, crude, bullying and stupid. He tweets
and lies incessantly, spends more time on golf
than briefing papers. Our Prime Minister is ordinary,
but his ordinary sentences are cut, shaped, polished
and dispensed in pre-assembled lengths. 'Go Sharkies!
How good is this! Jobs, jobs, jobs!'
It's hard to make sense, know what's forfeit,
in all this clamour. It's walking blindfolded
back and forth on a zebra crossing as cars
whoosh by from all directions sounding horns,
and past and present replicate or fade. It seems unlikely
the meek will inherit the earth.

Death has come among us. It has no need to hide,
disdains disguise. It ghosts across the fallen trees,
drifts downstream on the flood. It's in the gentle fog,
the shaft of sunlight on the range, the glistening
of the leaves, the magnolia in full bloom.
It's in the laughter of the impish boys and girls,
the chainsaws and the dozers, the trees clinging on.
In Missy hissing at what she cannot see.
It has no need to hurry, it does things by degrees,
by every shuddering breath, each shuffling step,
by unspoken words which ever are unspoken.
Scattered flowers for a shroud. Cedar for remembrance.
An orange moon swells in the eastern sky.

After floods and storms and lightning strikes,
we reinforce slopes which have washed away,
pry fallen trees from where they've flopped
into the river, bring down severed trunks
which have crashed into adjacent canopies:
you hear the rasp of bark against bark
as they shift and tighten. We cut the trunks
into lengths, set some aside for firewood,
stack rubbish to be burnt when weather permits.
It will all be ash. The mind must think
of other things, the cloud of gnats lifting
and sifting between the shrubs, the long-legged insects
skittering on the river, spiders' webs
so finely strung. A kingfisher who has spied fish-splash
beneath the wispy cloud and flickering light.
We put some human order into what is already ordered
in its own green tangle, an earthy rough sublime cut to size.
Cockatoos punch holes in tangelos brimming on the tree.

It appears Van Gogh spent his last day
painting tree roots that clung to a steep embankment
on Rue Daubigny. Surprisingly, and unsurprisingly,
they're blue. They twist and jut and overlap.
They look like bones. Somehow they are substantial –
gripped by and gripping the hard-mud earth. And fragile –
thin, knobbly, vulnerable. Daubed clumps of greenery
are the quickly painted over-story. The roots, the under,
and under-that story. They strain against each other,
depend upon each other, each reminding us
to pay attention. Momentarily denying time.

Undiminished

Grief is a flightless bird. Its antedated wings
are clasped around you and there is
pitiless assurance in the yielding feathers
and warm, substantial body whose embrace
holds you as though you were a day-old chick.

Weightless, you would rise above the cloud
but, for now, this enfolding is proof of tenderness,
that sorrow is still powerful, its sting alive:
the crushing hug, that sideways glance, the way she had
of being present even when far away.

You are a bewildered insect entombed
at the centre of a spider's web. Its vibrating strings
play no earthly tune in the darkness of the night

where stars pulse and fade in fathomless time
and beauty hides. It is latent in the bird,
in web, stars, in memory undiminished.

Contra Lorca

Dawn in Clovelly brings birdsong, the sweet and the shrill
tuning their instruments, playing their parts …

and the deep blue hour before dawn turns golden
as Eos, saffron-cloaked, rosy-fingered god,
scatters colour across the sky. Her tears
glisten on the grass. Soon the gates of heaven
will be opened to the sun. Dawn in Clovelly …

sleek, black and pleated, magpies and ravens
perch on gravestones and crosses like canopic urns.
They spy on each other side-eyed as the sun
splits the horizon's taut, blue rim. It strikes angels,
monks and madonnas, rouses them from night's cold sleep …

Venus and Jupiter still visible to the naked eye
of a boy walking barefoot through the cemetery
pushing a pram. Dawn in Clovelly …

and rosellas thread their fierce colours
through grevillea blooms; crimson and cream filaments
explode like stars. Dawn in Clovelly …

and garbage trucks startle and wheeze,
the newspaper sails over our front fence
and lands in the yard with a thump,
a motor bike chokes, growls and purrs,
three kookaburras cackle on a telephone wire,
a child cries …

dogs gambol and tug at their leads, joggers jog,
lovers hold hands, surfers slip under waves,
slip into air again, as we are submerged

in this altogether worldly light.

A shaft of sunlight
escapes the cloud,
shatters on rocks.

Joe Palooka

You wake in the half-light before dawn with the realisation
your past is a dream ...

There is a temptation to tell someone
but you won't ...

This might be privacy, or a conviction that listeners
would be as uninterested as they are in re-told dreams.
Or it might be that you are at peace with your past,
nothing to visit here ...

The past comes back stuttering, backlit
and un-sequenced like slides rattling and sticking
in an old-fashioned carousel:

A scene with a dog you can't recall, children in cashmere,
three-quarter pose, awkward in a photographer's studio,
a paddling pool made of canvas that leaks and falls apart,
a cubby house clasped in the branches of a tree, a tarantula
trapped in your fire-red hair. A life size, inflatable

Joe Palooka doll which bounces up
whenever you knock it down, a cowboy
with chaps and pistols holstered on each hip, a mother
who is dying in a room down the hall.

It comes to you that future and past can be interchanged.
You can't help but remember other pasts, just as you
dream brighter futures. Each presses hard on the present.

Voltage Across a Membrane

A ringing in the ears that could be cicadas
or tinnitus. Outside, the muted din of silence,
inside the silence of isolation. Flowering eucalypts

peer in at the window as the clouds
look down on them. A bird settles on a branch,
his cheep breaks the silence. A hammer falls on wood,

a child's voice pipes excitedly but indecipherably,
a plane and a car cast their sounds to the air.
Things move on, forward, but isolation remains the same:

the shape of the body in a small space.
The loud silences of the mind doing calisthenics
in the arena of the skull. Kettlebells, dumbbells,

barbells flung into space, dropped to the ground
with a thud and an awareness of breath
in the nostrils, in the throat, in the lungs, the outside

coming in and going out raggedly to keep the body
in this confinement. A leaf falls from the tree and spirals
unevenly down. Then another. Then no more.

Leaves cling to their branches and twigs as the wind
swishes them here and here, together and in isolation.

Ptolemy could define the earth in eight thousand
discrete points. Macrobius depicted a round, schematic world,
Terra Australis nondum cognita assumed to be. From his cell,

Frau Mauro stitched sailors' tales into his projections,
then declared, 'it now exists'. James Cook, on the other hand,
could approximate latitude thirty-nine within a mile, his maps,

accurate, proportionate, a precision of India ink.
Out to sea, waves run before the wind; nearer shore
fish striped black and gold like tiny Bengal tigers

fidget nervously through the weed, long-nosed
silver garfish sweep in a billowing cloud,
and the groper, far below, grazes massively among the shells.

What holds all this together? Where is the thread?
And now, ambiguously, rain marks its presence
against the glass in imagined rhythms, tones and glottal stops,

in blobs and runs. I see children skylarking,
swimming like speckled fish through its ribbons.
They pick blossoms from the trees, lasso clouds,

exchange songs with the birds, greetings with the wind.
They wave to me through the window and I sing
of an empty room, of silence, of a lack

for nothing in this moment, in this room,
of the mismatched joys of inertia and peripeteia.
Does 'need' imply both design and destination?

What is compulsion except the need to go on? Is it a search for equilibrium
or its denial? A demonstration of the second law of thermodynamics?
That's going too far:

stretching a milestone moment in physics and turning it into
a cheap poetic trick. The limitations of my thinking, the boundaries

against which it butts! Entropy indeed! I start again. I start again.
I close my eyes. I look out the window, I walk along the cliff edge,
my feet pressing firmly on rock, lifting easily into air, going

where I cannot. And I'm trying to make something out of this, something
which it is not. It's windy today, overcast and gusty, difficult

to make out clouds amongst the many shades of grey
except when they are harried by wind
and their edges become ragged like fraying carpet.

༘

Duty and desire dance around each other
like evenly-matched boxers in a makeshift ring.

Their booted feet shuffle on the canvas as they feint,
duck, swerve, cover-up to absorb imagined blows.

There is no blood, no spittle, no sweat. It could be virtual
but for the ragged breathing, the grunts, the sudden

expulsions of air. Is this shape without pattern, style
without substance or something else entirely? The refusal of meaning

doesn't mean that meaning fails to exist. That aphoristic quip
is self-conscious, its bravado disguises unease,

what I have neglected to disclose. The sea has no itinerary,
no intention. Nor do the trees though, in their way,

they each keep time, more or less like planets
circling the sun, twisting on their axes.

Neither have they intimacy or objective. Thinking about it —
shedding leaves and bark, soaking into sand, slapping at cliffs —

matter at once scatters and coheres. This room
makes space, is spacious within its confines.

It encourages perambulation. I take my mind for a walk,
sense proportions, look out for junctures

and hints of filiation. Sitting at looms
in Pakistan and Afghanistan women weave stories

into carpets being born beneath their hands. Refugees
huddle in tents, wrap their feet in rags, stare at border fences.

In 430 BC, Thucydides tells us, plague devastated Athens.
It killed Pericles. And one third of the population. In 1665

the rich fled London to escape the plague. Left behind to die
were their retainers, domestic servants and the poor.

What can 'alone' mean without a context?

What would it mean for Eurydice, for those solo
round-the-world sailors, for the crossers
of the Arctic on skis, for the lone explorers in that vast time
before phones, viral networks, global positioning satellites?

They're talking to themselves, listening for echoes,
sensing a something swirling outside the compass
of their conversation. Is this comforting or a threat?

Is there a plot in 'isolation'? When does the action begin?
(The instant bleeds into the hour, the hour into the day.)
We minor characters cling precariously to our lines,
and 'story', barely begun, casts round for its end.

A magpie dangles a worm from her sharp beak.
Does she have babies squabbling and screeching in a nest?
Can she know that a divided worm may become two,
two two-headed worms, two two-tailed worms?

In one sense this is true: life is voltage across a membrane.

You can see I keep shifting the argument,
but I'm trying hard to see what it is
that I'm not seeing, that flickering thing
whose seed is in itself. Does being directed to 'stay at home'
make 'home' an uncreated thing? Where is home
for the spared, the forgiven, the persecuted and forgotten?
What might time mean for them?

When time has ceased to have meaning,
Voyager may still be flying inter-stellar space,

its destination, a globular cluster twenty thousand
light years distant. On board, our voices, histories,
conversations, our equations, drawings, songs,

all the things that make us 'us'. Will anyone out there
understand what we, in our isolation, barely comprehend?

The eremite in his cave
wants for nothing,
is given nothing.

Between Time

You wake in the sleeping car of a speeding train …

The landscape flashes by in chunks,
hour upon hour, glacial and supersonic,
massing on the horizon …

crumbling homes, rusting tractors, abandoned cars, clouds cumulus
and nimbus, stream past the window …

Your compartment is virtually a world.

You have everything you need. A flop-down bed,
a pop-out, copper basin, an attendant who brings food
at uncertain intervals. Another who calls, 'Tickets, please!'
and excites a many-fingered fumbling in your pockets
for tickets you can never find.

The world beyond the window may be virtual, too,
an unchanging-ever-changing movie set. You stare at it
expecting something significant like a rifle shot
or bushrangers on horseback, desert fathers, camels
plodding nose to tail, but nothing has shown up yet.

Head braced against the glass you're nodding off again.

You think you have been on this train for days,
it might be weeks, you don't know if it is running on time.
Dimly, you remember the station where you embarked.

You're becoming unsettled as you realise you're uncertain
where you're headed or when you're expected to arrive.

The Traveller Reminisces

See us / if you will, hair to our shoulders,
beards to our chests, wearing kaftans, dhotis,
djellabas, pherans, leather coats lined with karakul,
bracelets at our wrists, Jesus sandals on our feet.

We're smoking dope in Kathmandu, opium in Laos,
scoring smack in Casablanca, yage in the Amazon,
hanging out with sadhus on the ghats, hill tribes
in the jungles, shaking hands with Carlos Castaneda.

We've fuzzy memories of Angkor Wat, riding donkeys
in the Valley of the Kings, climbing Tiger Mountain
to see sunrise on Kanchenjunga, watching turtles
hatch in Terengganu, selling whiskey in Rangoon.

Do you remember, diarrhoea in Delhi, dysentery in Denpasar,
that rotten meat from the butcher in Darjeeling, liver
from a Cairo stall, that train we missed in Ankara,
sleeping on the station, sleeping on the steps

of the Taj Mahal, pressed into a doorway in Jerusalem
as soldiers cleared the streets, call girls in Bangkok,
Pathan warriors, rifles on their backs, bandoliers
across their chests, guarding the foot of the Khyber Pass?

Here is a coast; here is a harbour; here a hotel,
here a ruin, there a river, there a mosque,
now a castle, then a cathedral, next a museum,
not another Saxon keep! Where will we sleep tonight?

See us / if you will applying sunscreen, sporting floppy hats,
popping medication, sauntering the promenade
in sensible walking shoes, sanitising our hands
before each and every meal; we're drinking beer

in Bali, Noosa and Byron Bay, trading reflections
in our mirrored glasses, comparing package deals.
We're tapping at a door marked 'perception',
forever disappointed there's no one home.

My bald head
is dreaming
rainforest trees.

Letter to Tristram Shandy, Gentleman

Sir,
From the incalculable distance of this century,
I beg you excuse my temerity in daring
to insert my considerable whim-wham into
your life and opinions. My threadbare excuse,
miserable as it is, and certainly incommensurate
with the offence, is unbounded admiration
for your accomplishment — who but you
could stop-up his own birth until chapter twenty-six
or twenty-seven of volume lll — and acknowledgement
of my own stuttering pen-craft. Zounds, to be able
to go full tilt down the byways and alleys, tracks
and deviations with but a passing raspberry
for the highway and a resounding fart
for the criticks. Your reputation, your life as such,
put in jeopardy by words. Why, Sir, such panache
must be praised in the most effusive terms.
Oh, to be be-virtu'd, be-pictur'd, be-butterflied,
and be-fiddled, progressive and digressive
successively and all at once! Humbly
may I beg a boon, could you, admired Sir,
but pen a brief endorsement for my own
undeserving volume which, presumptuously, I have enclosed.

Big-Time Wrestling

Charles Simic and Mary Oliver leap into the ring.
It's the semi-finals of World Championship Poetics
and there's a Pulitzer up for grabs. They're keen.

They circle warily looking for a metaphor, a symbol.
Oliver throws out a bear, a snake, a deer, a gannet.
Simic ducks, feints, counters with The Black Queen,

a pig and an angel, naked nymphs, a six-legged dog,
a red pencil, empty streets at sundown, a grin.
Oliver staggers, almost falls, one hand on the canvas.

To catch her breath she walks a forest glade, a meadow.
Lounging on the ring's perimeter, Simic sips chilled wine.
It tastes like a woman's glove, a dusty shoe.

He signals to his corner and a spirit in fancy dress
appears to re-fill his glass. Oliver swoops, pelts Simic
with peonies, goldenrod, pine needles, lilies, blueberries,

marigolds, poppies, whelks, a swan, a humpback whale.
'Have you ever dared to pray?' she hisses in his ear, as Simic,
stumbles, spills his wine and, through bloodied gums,

can only mumble, 'Hardly a day passes, but sometimes
Gods dress as nuns or waitresses or the Devil and there's always
shadows or black wings.' 'Snow,' says Oliver, 'waterfall, river, blossoms.'

'Sidewalks, alleyways, cellars, Eighth Avenue,' Simic whispers
as he squeezes her in a clinch. For ten rounds they fight like this,
like Heaven versus Hell until, at a standstill,

spent, they are panting in their respective corners.

The crowd is silent now, the judges have conferred, the referee strides to centre ring, reaches for the microphone, announces ...

Culture

It starts off as a walk around the block,
an I-do-this, I-do-that kind of diversion,
aimless but pleasant, the accepted, expected
encounters with sky and sea, dogs doing their do.
Then a gap where a home once was, an open mouth
from which a front tooth has been abruptly punched.
The long-standing bungalow, its foundations undermined,
is re-thought, re-engineered, re-painted so it emerges
almost beyond recognition: the aged humanist in his castle
under siege; the Enlightenment cast into darkness;
the old touchstones — reason, liberty, beauty — suspected
of being double agents of privilege and power.
Which they may be. It's hard to tell on a walk.

The dandelion's puffball
is undisturbed
when scattered on your breath.

On or About December 1910

It's a day for idling. Autumn, mild, warm,
blue sky, just a breath of wind to remind you
winter is on its way. There's no pressing need

to do anything much, just think, wonder,
enjoy the weather on your skin. You don't hear
'idling' much these days. It's a word in danger

of dropping from the lexicon. I'm not even sure
cars idle any more. Maybe, like us, they're more likely
to procrastinate. Like me. I've been meaning

to re-read Bertrand Russell's essay, 'In Praise of Idleness'
but I never seem to find the time, or it's never
the right time and, I admit, I'm a little afraid I might

have misremembered it. It's encouraging, then, to remember
Russell lamented only a handful of people had ever read
Principia Mathematica cover to cover and only two

had understood it. A bit like poetry though,
you understand, I'm not comparing my stuff to Russell's.
Anyway, I'm not sure I could find it on my shelves,

stuffed with foxed and yellowing paperbacks, Penguins
and the like which make me sneeze when I pick them up.
There was a time for idleness back then, especially

if you were from the aristocratic or intellectual class,
Bloomsbury and all that, Vita Sackville-West,
Virginia Woolf, Keynes, T. S. Eliot and his wife.

Today they'd be on the cover of *New Weekly*
or some other disreputable rag. Breathless revelations
of their shenanigans, paparazzi snapping Woolf

in a room of her own. December 1910 approaches.
Then August 1914. The world is about to change. Nothing
will be the same, no time for idleness, ever again.

Velcro

Distinctions should be made. Idleness
is not boredom. This inaction, time without purpose,
is a gift. You wake up and it is luxurious to ask,
'What shall I do today?' and not expect an answer.
Not laziness but preparedness for what the day will offer.
The flâneur idling down a Parisian boulevard
is not bored. He is on the lookout, or attending
to who might be looking at him. Right now
I'm doodling and, paradoxically, this purposelessness
is purposeful. It is a way of finding out, so a speck
in an otherwise empty sky might be a UFO or a god
or just a bird; or a silver fish breaking the still, blue-black
surface of a lake becomes a skinny-dipping moon. Idling
is to be 'put in mind', it is musing married to movement,
and to the nine muses lollygagging on Mount Helicon.
It is a leaf spiralling in a quibbling breeze, a dance
whose steps are happily un-choreographed. Newton,
drowsing under an apple tree (I know this story
is likely apocryphal), would never have been struck
by gravity without this idleness. Many a scientist
looking for one thing has tumbled upon another.
Velcro and Viagra were discovered this way.
And LSD and play-doh. The pacemaker in my chest
is a chance side-effect of different research. Strictly,
it must be acknowledged this is accident, but perhaps
it is also the by-product of an idly-incubated mind.

Half the Sins

In *Conquest of Happiness*, Bertrand Russell
devotes a chapter to boredom which, for him,
is thwarted desire. He speculates (is it possible
he is serious?) that half the sins of mankind
are down to boredom or attempts to escape it.

Kierkegaard thought boredom equalled nothingness,
and Schopenhauer, that cheery soul,
thought boredom exposed the vanity of existence.
(Imagine what Schopenhauer would have said
of television, of iPhones, of the wittering of twitter.)

(I'm not sure, must I delineate acedia from ennui, and both
from Weltschmerz, all of which whiff of self-regard?)

Boredom isn't unrelentingly bad.
Like its second cousin idleness, boredom leaves space
for something else to fill. It's a Japanese stone garden,
vacancy to contemplate, to rake and rake again.
It's holding your breath and counting backwards
from one hundred before breathing out

and breathing in again. If I understand him correctly,
Heidegger quite liked boredom. It gives us,
he thought, access to time and being
undeceived by the masks of purpose and activity.

We're close to truth claims here, to what addled brains
used to claim for LSD. If unending,
boredom must be death but if, inevitably,
boredom must give way, it is precedence,
a cleansing of the mind for what comes next.

Posthumous Existence

You wake and don't know where you are ...

Nothing to worry about, this has happened before,
lie quietly, enjoy the momentary disorientation,
the familiar will recollect itself soon enough.

But nothing is changing. You seem to be simultaneously
awake and asleep, participant and observer,
your well-known body somehow insubstantial

as though you are in a hocus-pocus movie
where spirits exit bodies, the dead arise,
and the rules of the reasonable world don't apply.

Yet you are still thinking. Demonstrably so ...

At least you have the sensation of thought but,
so strange, so liminal is this suspension
you doubt even that. Are your eyes open or closed?

This is the borderlands and all you see,
stretching as far as you see, are drifts and dunes,
and shades shifting from yellow to ochre,
and then those strata of crimson which suggest

horizon, if 'horizon' applies to something so indistinct.

Is it possible you are crossing over, leaving behind
what is known and real for a future
which has never been promised or sought,

not even something imagined, not garden, or palace,
not wilderness, not sky or ocean, not even desert,
though 'desert' is all the mind will allow.

'Past' and 'future' have lost all meaning and, without them,
this present is impossible to define, just as you
cannot be defined. In the circumstances, is it silly

to keep worrying at the reach of eternity's span?

The kid on a billycart
is screaming down the hill,
a grin glued to his lips.

Self Portrait : Sea Scale

A man stands on the shoreline
facing the horizon. Light glances off
the unquiet, morning sea and his right arm
is crooked so he seems to be saluting, wrapt
and at attention. He casts a flat,
elongated shadow on the still cool,
gritty sand. It is as if the sun
has transfixed him: the bodily and unbodily
jointed at their heels. Something about
his upright substance and the prone shadow's
black absence suggests a space to be resolved.
The man stands this way a long time
but what he is thinking, what his gesture means,
remains unclear …

We all start out inside, attached,
denizens of a damp, dark world which alters
but stays the same as, floating with the currents,
we kick, wriggle and roll over, fish assuming
improvised and predetermined shapes and postures.
Is there, conceivably, a sense of self or time?
There must be touch, the nature of matter
against relenting and resisting matter,
but is there an awareness, incipient perhaps,
of cleavage which will never end?

I dive into the sea and know again
a difference from the air: a change of texture,
temperature, how the hole one makes in water

is apparent, as that in air is not.
Do seals notice this? Or penguins as they make
that funny, upright leap onto ice? Which element
do they take for granted, which is a surprise?

What could the man be looking at or for?
The 'boasted glories of the ocean,' Darwin declared
'a tedious waste, a desert of water.' This can't be,
though, for all its variety, its colours and depths,
its swells and troughs, the sea is mostly
a cloth of shades stretching to that false horizon,
the untouchable we are bound to surmise ...

The world as we know it is never still,

never the same as we knew it yesterday
or the day before, or when one was a child
and the world was a mystery we wondered about
or took for granted, so consumed I was

with football, with running fast, with the next wave,
the day to day of the classroom and the playground,
with marbles and red rover, with yo-yo tricks,
and whose turn it was to bat. And then, soon,
with this and that, the must, should, could, which steal time.

The light I see playing across the water is not the light
scudding across the surface when I look again.
Is that what the man is thinking? That time
is on the flood, running out, that perspective
changes everything, even time. That the sea,

stretched cliff to cliff, and from the shore
to beyond the horizon is of incommensurate scale.

The tide is ebbing, crabs are scuttling
crevice to crack and green weed is already
tinged brown and brittle. Seagulls at the water's edge
await an invisible signal to take flight ...

༄

The man's body begins to spin seemingly

of its own volition, a slow-motion dip and swirl,
arms out-stretched, in-drawn, and wrapped-around
as his torso twirls, twists, folds and looks to float
free of the sand to which his feet are fixed.

His shadow flutters too but it is diffident,
reserved. Uncertain of its role, it waits for cues.

It is a dance in imitation of the fluky wind,
the glancing light, the inclement sea's up-rising
and down-falling, an immersion or surrender

to the outside, the out-sized. Falteringly
we are and are not ourselves, conscious momentarily
of movement, momentarily unconscious. Meaning
is intrinsic but may be beside the point ...

༄

Thinking I become someone else and then
I am myself again, or I am myself and others jointly,
inventing conversations, thinking others' thoughts,
as if I were there, as if I were them, as if
I were looking into a mirror dimly aware
of a ghostly shadow behind my own. I know that man,

he resembles me but I can't determine
if he is 'was' or 'will be'. It's folly
to explain myself to myself, to hold up a mirror
like an artist eager for a self-portrait, to inspect
the imprint on the sand for clues. There's no doubt

I'll lie. Trim a little here, inflate a little there,
and beyond these little fictions what is it I really know?
'To paint water in all its perfection,' Ruskin wrote
'is as impossible as to paint the soul.'

The sea sloshes through my thoughts, my human cares.
Is it too fanciful to think that, swimming,
I am attached, inside, all muscle and flesh, almost naked,
my moderate body heaved sideways, borne up, borne down
by the immoderate sea, holding my breath as the white foam
surges above me or, provisionally in control, skidding across
a wave's green face; this time, this place, momentarily

 young again, weightless as the dancing man …

It's a noisy business, swimming:
    the beat of the legs, the slap, plunge, pull
        of the arms, the breath drawn in

and forcibly exhaled, the rising bubbles
    which look like they should pop, water burbling
        in the ears, the swivelling face snatching

glimpses of the sky, fuzzy impressions of the sand,
    the tock, tock, tock of slow time, the wavering voice
        of thought: the circling shark

of our imagination, the stingray, whale, Maori Wras,
    sea dragons, turtles, crabs; mermaids
        and mermen lolling on rocky foreshores;

and twenty-thousand leagues below
    the Nautilus locked in the curious grip
        of a giant squid. Do boys still dream

of being privateers and buccaneers? (Fifty years ago,
    to a class of pimply, landlocked fifteen year-olds,
        I played Debussy's 'La Mer' to enliven

their reading of HMS Ulysses. 'Stimulus Variation'
    it was termed in the hopeful jargon
        of the time. Its effect:

inattention, sucked-paper pellets flicked
    across the room, and a red-faced teacher
        praying for the bell.)

Low tide on New Year's Eve;
storms in the Coral Sea, low pressure in the Tasman;
opposed swells hurled onto the coast;

Bronte Beach awash. Waves churn,
leap, clump and thrash
fill up and stall,
thump on a shallow bank and of a sudden
rush parallel to the sand. The southern rip

ploughs a swathe through the waves
and whisks me towards the cemetery.
Waves bounce off the cliffs
and a second rip twists to Tamarama.

Careless, inattentive,
I've misjudged my strength, the sea's incoherence,
and struggle to swim against such frenzy.
Water has its way.

I'm dragged beyond the point, caught inside the break;
swirled around and tumbled
inside out and upside down,
white foam turning black around me.

The body, blotched and barnacled, freckled and scarred,
tugged every which way by the sea,
swallowed whole,

spat into the rip's impatient maw,
swept back out to sea, and the drowning nightmare
made far too potent.

Mind awry, feigning calm, I swim towards the reef,
                        grasp weed, clutch rocks,
                        gasp for breath,
            stumble and cut my belly and my shins
                    still the rip
                    would drag me off my feet.

Bushfire haze hangs above the beach,
                fireworks are charged and fused,
                and white-hulled boats cluster on the harbour
                      sails flapping …

I imagine the man watching deep sea swells
which bulge along the horizon, the leaping
and disappearing whitecaps which are wind,
the undulating backs of whales which are beauty,
the instinctive, ever-hopeful flight of the cormorant,
albatross, shearwater, gull, the material

miracle of phosphoresce. I imagine him
thinking of Magellan, James Cook, da Gama,
the many others sailing into the unknown
in bold, imperial boats no bigger
than a harbour ferry, challenging the seas,
succumbing to the seas (reefs and headlands
decorated by wrecks, the ocean floor bedecked),
charting coastlines to unmake the world;
he sees ghost ships plying their ghastly trades.

He's trying to remember Hokusai's Great Wave
and all its reproductions. Monet's fierce and

gentle seas, Gericault's Raft of Medusa,
Turner's one thousand indistinctions, Leonardo's
imagined bird's-eye view, as much map as painting.
They stare quizzically at him from gallery walls.

He's thinking of the Mariana Trench
and the unfathomable creatures surviving there,
the fiction of the Bermuda Triangle, the parable
of Captain Ahab, the Great Pacific Garbage Patch,
bigger than Texas, where plastic outnumbers plankton
ten to one, the retreating ice, bleaching coral,
where seas once were, will be. He thinks:

warming seas can't gasp for air — fish can ...

༃

In one drop of water

                                                            is found

                      a pale blue dot

a wolf

                       a lynx

                                         a hungry dog

                     the sea, the sea

                                    with uproar rude

tempest tossed

the depths, the depths

a strong green god

that grey vault

the wine dark sea

sighing like a sleeper　　　　　　　　　*the vast emptiness*

teeming with life

from outer space

the endless ocean …

The man is leaving now. I watch him turn from the sea
and trudge, trance-like and small, towards the promenade
and what it demarks.

Have I invented him, his thoughts, what he sees
and what he leaves behind? Whose eyes
have I borrowed to let him see?

Surfer's eye, surface eye, fiction's eye?
Landman's eye: always looking 'at',
not 'in', 'on' or 'under', prepositions
which make all the difference.

So many eyes, so many seas, oceans,
bays, basins, inlets, straits, passages,
currents, channels, tides, gutters,
holes, banks, rips, ripples,
capes, cliffs, fjords, promontories:
it's impudent to skip words off the sea.

We live against the ocean, snuggled up, clustered round.
Yet build bulwarks against its presence,
boardwalks, seawalls, breakwaters, piers, jetties.
So water chafes, rubs, slaps and grinds.
We dredge its harbours, sink wells into its floors,
splash oil across its unsuspecting waters,
drag fish protesting from its depths.

All this is true. Confessed. But still the sea, eternal,
one prays eternal, ending and re-starting,
running in and running out, wet and heaving,
not one drop spilt as the earth tilts on its axis,
spins at breakneck speed around the sun.
The sea where, after all, it all began.

What unfolds here, unfurls, is grace
(On a branch / floating downriver /
a cricket singing). I give thanks
for joys which come unbidden,
which cradle the uncommodified body
in a caress which could as easily kill.
I will take the devil's deal for more of this,
for the dance, the sounding beauty, knowing always,
that I will surely end.

and dug my fingers in the sand
(2000)

and dug my fingers in the sand

1. Monday
In the squeeze and thrust of its uprising
the stunned face of the Great Dividing Range
twists and grinds impassively in stone.
Once wild rivers – Snowy, Shoalhaven, Clyde –
still sweep the rock through channelled hills down
to the slow decline of the continental shelf.
Here the quartz is washed, puddled and abraded,
sinks to the wedged foot of weed, becomes a bed for shells,
a shifting yellow paddock for herds of browsing fish.
Unaware, before-dawn fishermen fling
invisible lines into a creaseless sea,
settle to a tight hypotenuse
of anticipation, lean back against the air
and haul the idea of the sun from the flat horizon
like a red, reluctant mountain peak.
Its first scudding light splits clouds, skims like flat stones
over the surface of the sea and ricochets
around the beach and Christian clifftop monuments.

2. Tuesday
In the slant light I swim lengths of a narrow bay,
out towards the horizon, the sky, and the sun
that hangs hovering like a hypnotist's medallion,
then back, again and again, to the low-slung beach.
Below me weed swirls and the sand shuffles
in the cold current that moved inshore last night.
I'm in the sea but not of it, neither fish
nor fisherman nor sailor with their understanding
of its distance and its depths, displaced
like Archimedes, divided by a Plimsoll line,

floating on the surface, a spaceman in my mask,
trying to tell which alien fish is which
and what the difference is between their stripes and colours.
There's no gravity here and I must dive deliberately
to sort out the grammar of their sunken lives.
Stretched on the stones, his grey-domed body wider
than my curved arms, a stingray lies motionless and strange,
not even a flap of his wide skirt or interest in his eye
to signify my presence, just a retinue
of transparent fish and the tapered spike of tail.
I climb up bubbles and break back into air.

3. Wednesday

The tide rises with the sun and just as slowly.
Rocks submerge and the sea's transcribed in the slap
of waves against the sloping sand, the wet print of gulls
and the calligraphy of children on the shore.
On an outside bank the sea lines up as light
and boardriders split the face of waves then sink
into the swollen water of the rip. Smaller than a bird
a plane trails smoke across the sky more slowly
than re-appearing blue absorbs the signs and sound.
The fishing boats are back already, resting on their slats
or raised like totems on their sterns. The knives of men
slice silver skin and spray the scale like offerings.
From the lighthouse I watch a sunfish and his court of dolphins
swim north beyond the point while the unseen current
scatters a cloud of sand as it continues in their wake.

4. Thursday

Flags droop against their poles and a shadow
circles round my feet. All the marinaded men
and women, the zinc-creamed boys and girls,

basted with sweat and oil, smelling of coconut
and Hawaiian Spice, salted, baked, browned or burnt,
stretch on beach-towel grills under the sun's rotisserie eye.
Surfers loll motionless on boards. Seagulls congregate
below the cliffs for shade, taps and iceblocks drip
and all along the coast we're drawn down to that rubbed,
south-sea rolled mountain quartz, the refined white powder
of Hyams Beach, the antic yellow grit of Byron Bay,
all swept flat or shimmering like low desert waves.
Nothing moves. The sea's an introverted lens
of sticky light, the sky its own high, taut reflection,
just a few lean clouds scrolled on the rim's quick edge.

5. Friday

It's been blowing from the south all day: storm surf.
swells writhe to axe-edge peaks, teeter, tear and fall,
their slipstream spray tattered by afternoon wind.
Their grip is sharp and cold. I've caught waves, I swear,
two storeys high, kicked off on that sudden skidding drop,
balanced, too late for choice, between excitement and the fear.
Alone in the sea, I've dived under waves that closed
like fists around me, felt their shock reverberate
from cliffs, and watched the white foam flex towards me.
I held my breath and dug my fingers in the sand. It tore me up
and flung me down until I couldn't tell which was which
and thought I was about to drown. But this,
this really speaks of death and I'm older now and frightened –
the bay is overfull of spilling crests and water ripping in and out.
They say south coast tidal waves washed boulders miles inland
seven thousand years ago. I can well believe it. I've seen waves
leave rocks as big as gravestones on the beach and heap
an unfamiliar topography of hills above the promenade.

6. Saturday

The still-stalling sun and premature street light overlap
the smell of backyard barbecues, the hotel's rising amber din
and the long, lagging strokes of an evening swimmer
trying to catch water running through splayed hands.
The fishermen have returned, casting their arcs
into a sea ironed flat and slick by the heat of day.
Dull lead draws lines down, cork floats in shadowed light
and careless fish are jerked suddenly into empty air.
Couples stroll and a man stands at the breakwater gazing east.
The beach is waste with plastic, weed, forgotten towels
as the late tide gently tugs loose sand back out to sea.
In the last light that strikes the cliff, grains of quartz
stand out and it's hard to tell if they've been subject
to centuries of decay or just begun to form
the limit of this chafed line of rise and fall.

7. Sunday

Narrabeen Lagoon and Myall Lakes, rippled and asleep,
are knuckled from the sea by sand. A middling moon
sows their neat, wind-run furrows with seeds of light.
Once they were beaches but the restless, constant sea,
tides, winds, the southern current, sealed their nights
for dreams of dinghies grazing at the end of loose-looped ropes.
To the east, beyond the shallows of the continental shelf
lie deep submarine trenches where eyes protrude on stalks,
fish navigate by touch, jellyfish glow and grotesques
float up like uncalled fears and sink half-forgotten with the dawn.
By the movement of the seas our margins are revised. If they fall,
the land will domesticate the sea. If they rise, lake and lagoon
will be beaches once again and the flooding of Barrenjoey spit
will pitch waves against the sandstone cliffs of West Head
and leave a lighthouse squinting from an island in the sea.

Physical

You step off the edge of a pool, a springboard, a cliff,
a world, into the brief, lingering drop through the air, absence
then presence in the splash and broken liquid skin, the blue nano-second
in-and out-ness before the materiality of water,
the disturbance, the slap, lap, leap and splash of it, the settlement,
the elastic, amniotic embrace of it and in the sinking
and slowing, the push, pull, float and hold, you understand
displacement and Newton's first, second and third laws, in those
spherical bubbles making for the surface you think you might
define the other and the self, in the ripple and run
and fall of water down the length of your side, in the pressure
and pitch, the slip, sweep, swell and wash, in the motion and mass,
the catch, thrust, heave, lift and roll of arm, in that rare moment,
you know what it is to be a fish. Or a lion. Or a bird.
It's like those last shuddering seconds of love before the lag
and the drag and the inkling of what entropy might possibly be.

Song of Songs 5 : 2

I wake too early, too late, unmoored before dawn.
Sleep won't come back. I listen to the populated dark,
try to give shape to the sounds I hear. They must be
insects, birds: I can't get nearer than that. I try
to give form to thoughts, observe them
as they trail from hiding place to hiding place
or prod them if they refuse to move, head and tail
pulled in, the thin shell that could so easily
crack. Memory comes embodied: she has your shy and
sudden smile, her breath against my ear is yours, the moon
and apples are on her lips and at her neck the rise
and rise of pulse is yours, is mine. My slow hands trace
the outline of your spine, the small of, swell and shiver of
new morning skin, and hold you in this light dark.
I may have drowsed
                        but my heart was never more awake.

Cowboys

The garden seat was made of busted slats
and rusted iron, it curved behind my calves
and spine like waves. It was a ship in childhood games,
home base and, because we'd painted it orange and black,
a tiger that we hunted or we fled. Upside down
it was a covered wagon the cowboys hid behind.
When my mum died I sat in the backyard
on the edge of the garden seat. No one told me
she was dead but the bedroom door was closed
and there were too many adults in the house
walking softly, talking softly and a black limousine
parked on the hill outside. My aunt, who was not
my aunt, put her arm around my shoulders and told me
it was all right to cry. All right to cry.
Her funeral was in a sandstone church between
the tramway cutting and the cliffs, the wind
blew in from the sea so hard my eyes stung
as I stood there in a white shirt and tie,
on the grass with the cowboys, with nothing to say.

My Father's Eyes

A webbing belt and polished brass contain the stomach
of his sergeant's uniform. Above a clipped moustache
his eyes present themselves uncertainly for inspection.

*

He smiles across the haberdashery counter uncarding lace,
counting buttons, wrapping fifteen-denier stockings in brown paper,
takes two and sixpence and wishes another customer good-day.

*

On stage as president of the amateur swimming club
he stands erect, eyes fixed on the wall behind our heads,
and sings God Save The Queen loudly and off key.

*

Steam rises from the thermos in his hands as he watches our mother
plant flowers round the fountain the P and C has built
at our primary school. We cut our names in wet cement.

*

He looks into the Box Brownie to take a picture in our backyard.
Mother sits on a tartan rug watching us roll around. Her mother,
in an oyster satin frock and elastic hose, keeps her eye on him.

*

Years since our mother's death he sits at the kitchen table
after the late news, dealing hands of patience into midnight,
eyes down on the cards that keep falling from his hands.

*

In his Reuben F Scarf suit he's folded down into the space
of the mini-minor, packed in with pamphlets and collection boxes;
my father's eyes enclosed in the oblong of the rear view mirror.

*

Cumbersome with a borrowed video camera that didn't work
he steps from the plane in Grafton for my wedding squinting in the heat
and aviation fuel. When we drive away next day his eyes are red.

*

In his new house he drinks a glass of sherry after work
and blinks against the cigarettes he's just begun to smoke again.
On the mantlepiece above his head a nautilus and line of smaller shells.

*

When I was twenty-four I said, "See you later,"
as though I was going down the street not overseas.
I looked down and didn't hold Dad's eyes, I didn't say good-bye.

Shellac

My grandmothers, both of them, both widows,
lived in dull rooms, a flat behind our house,
a flat above a draper's shop. Of my father
and my mother, they separately disapproved.
Mother and father didn't say a word
to me. Gran dressed in navy blue and wore
her grey hair in a bun. Nan favoured pastels —
oyster, cream — and kept her hair tightly permed.
They both wore glasses, endured arthritis,
and tapped old walking sticks, one black, one brown.
At Sunday dinners we had to sit up straight,
not fidget, not giggle at the silence.
I don't remember either of their deaths.
All their furniture was dark, the wardrobes,
Jacobean dressing tables, sideboards,
the skirtingboards and architraves: shellac.

*Female beetles, Laccifer lacca, secrete
trnmsparent gum, encase themselves on bark,
give birth and die (but how do the young get out?).
The amber jubes, dried, pulverised to flakes,
cut with alcohol, painted on and polished
in countless patient layers, give lacquerwork
a high, protective sheen. Thickly applied
it seals off insulates, and baffles light.*

Today I scrape back stain, work at it
with a blade, apply caustic, heat skirtingboard

with an open flame. I'm trying to get back
to raw wood. I work quietly, self-absorbed,

build up around me fragments, scraps. Behind me
my children crawl, hands busy with the shavings,

shellac sticking to their knees.

With My Father-in-Law

1. Akuna Bay

You get there going backwards
in a rowboat,
spine to the rising sun
bent forward in prayer
stretched back in praise;
at each wooden stroke
the blade chops blue glass
to wet strings in the sharp light,
and you lurch a little this way
and that, butting blindly
between the tall masts
impatient to sweep
in straight white lines
and beat the sun
to its western shore.

2. The Church Point Ferry

        It's timetabled,
though it doesn't matter if you're late
rounding Scotland Island with its wharves
reflected on Pittwater like cycle spokes,
no rim but the sea.
       At one,
a solemn-eyed boy strips to his underpants,
leaps into the ferry's whitewashed wake
and sinks; he splashes up laughing,
and floats on his back to shore.
       At another,

a man wades in up to his chin, submerges —
a Hindu in the Ganges — then rises
like a star; a barefoot girl sleeps upright
while seaweed creeps along her line.
                        The ferry
ruminates across the bay digesting water and time,
seagulls drift and graze on glints of sunlight,
a man lies down to paint his yacht, a barge rusts,
rowboats grey
                and I'd gladly pay the ferryman twice
to carry us round a second time.

3. Coal and Candle Creek

Coal and Candle Creek transmits
a bright morse code of light, and nothing
disturbs its equanimity.

Not the cruiser churning on its stern
to lift and drive the sharp peaked bow,
not the geometry of nylon lines
levering fish to flap in the giggling
hands of slippery boys and girls,
not the bitumen road that imitates
its shape through curves and hills.
Grandfather sits in the autumn sun,
helps us drag his woollen sweater off,
lies back in thermal underwear.

He's got too much skin, it collects
on the back of hands, at wrists, under eyes
(swept-up sand or dried and pleated weed),
his creased fingernails are lobster claws,

his veins like purple tubers twist, run
and swell beneath the puckered skin,
currents of unease twitch down his arms
and, from the acutely angled sun,
he shades his eyes as best he can. His face
is weathering like a sandstone cliff.

By night another load of sand is moved,
another root appears above the soil,
a few small rocks slide down the bank and sink
while Coal and Candle Creek leaks out to sea.

4. Narrabeen Lagoon

My dad died when I was twenty-five
(I wasn't there; my mum had died before).
The heart attack that killed him
left him little time to age, or me to fret.
Life just stopped on that sudden note.

My father-in-law is dying by degrees.
I watch him through his daughter's eyes,
middle-aged themselves by now.
Death takes its time playing out his song
note by note: the words are first to go.

He's left with gestures and his daughter
must imagine phrases in his eyes
and hope he understands when she responds.
He moves slowly now with frequent stops
and memory flickers on and off, he's here, he's not.
But oh, he knows too well this unremitting tune,
the strain to smile when all he wants to do is cry.

He's aged; his daughter grieves, her mother too;
and love, though strong, proves helpless near the end.

5. Alzheimers Wing

As insubstantial as torn cicada wings,
their old bodies are shot through with light,
the fallen leaves of autumn blown loose,
adrift and swaying in a fluky breeze of
incomprehension and the moment's present.
The once beautiful boys in uniforms
and photographs, the doctor, general,
ex-headmaster, larrikins and wits,
sunny as spring and smiling, now stand
in tracksuit pants and food dashed shirts,
shuffle corridors and sitting rooms,
gather against the locked glass door,
uneasy ghosts in waiting, in search of home,
lost beds, watches, false teeth, cigarettes,
wives, daughters, memories, reasons why.
They play games or sit in vinyl chairs and snooze.
Sun through afternoon and picture windows
paints haloes on their heads, stipples skin
stretched on frames of bone, the light and shade
of our benevolent confinement.

Crossing The Border

You step into Gould's bookshop, Newtown,
like a tourist crossing a border,
a literary traveller leaving the safelands behind
for the seedier streets —
as far removed from Dymocks
as Kathmandu from Kew.
It's hard to get your bearings here,
there's no Baedeker to trust
and the single sheet directory
 found at the door plots
a deceitful map of the territory.
Strange things are apt to happen
as you trek through aisles of travel
and climb corridors of lit. crit.
Books close in behind you, shadows shift,
volumes of verse slide beneath you and you jump
when you step on Noam Chomsky uncomplaining on the floor.
If you dare to draw a book from an upper shelf,
risking burial under an avalanche of paper,
you're overwhelmed to find rows behind rows,
endless Russian dolls and Chinese puzzles of words.
How will you ever know this land,
so mysterious, so beautiful, so strange?
Perhaps you'll never leave, now you've
gone native, bookwrecked on an alien shore.

Infidelity

In the course of a long marriage
I've been unfaithful to my wife
many times, though I hasten to add,
only with one woman and then
only in literature, never in real life,
and it should be pointed out
that my mistress pre-dates my wife
having taken my virginity at fifteen
reading by torchlight under the bedclothes
as surely as she took young Frederick's
on page 140 after the Bal des Quat' z' Arts.
She walked out of my life as out of Frederick's,
Kiki of Montparnasse, but not forever
though it was ten years before I found her again
remaindered in Gould's on Goulburn Street
not walking the Boul' Mich'
or drinking in the Jockey or the Dôme –
I was fifty years too late for that appointment
and probably still too shy to have spoken,
despite having been introduced by Hemingway
and having seen her, by this time frequently,
with Kisling, Utrillo, Foujita and others.
Though Man Ray and Brassai could not be denied
I never allowed the camera or the slim nineties
to distort imagination's sharp, soft image
of that lost generation, left behind by torchlight.

Improvising With Flaubert

1.
*If you put the sun inside your trousers, all you do
is burn your trousers and wet the sun.*

There's a ludic sky sweeping towards us and away
and the sea is realised in gooseflesh sound. It digs
as if to bury some horror on the beach.
                                                Boys in baggy shorts
and surf-permed hair scrabble along the sand,
heads bent against the wind, tips of noses turning blue.
Their toes examine a dead fish now swollen like a bladder
pumped too full of gas, eyes popped as if in fear
or knowledge.
                      This rain falls invisibly, erupts in pools
like white frogs jumping, then the intermingling
of concentric rings. They shiver and cross over
to contentment, the unseen surface tension, the weight
of shallow depths.
                         There's a memory of rain on tin roofs,
repeated notes of different frequency
and duration, a comfort to be inside
but a prison nonetheless.
                            In the distance lightning strikes,
white veins fork beneath clenched skin.

2.
*Absolute doubt now seems to me so completely substantiated
that it would be almost silly to seek to formulate it.*

The air's made visible by heat, the humming contours
of summer, or by its absence: plate glass winter's
white refractions and obscurities of fog.
                              Oswald Spengler
lamented the modern world, thought it uncaring,
predatory, a despotism of sight which separates all this
from that.

            Isaac Newton counted seven colours in the spectrum
to translate harmony into light and the Albert Hall
once boasted an organ to pump out colour with each sound.
We hear two notes simultaneously as one but register
their difference. Superimpose blue on yellow
and we see only green.

                    When Ganesh is carved in stone
his eyes stay closed till last. They're opened with music
and decorated mallets and he's consecrated with milk,
vermilion. In the Book of Job friends who come to witness
sit silently for seven days.

                        Which would you rather be,
we ask as children, deaf or blind, and I refuse to answer.
I wonder what it would be like not to think or feel or
to subtract one sense at a time

                        until we were only matter.

3.

Language is like a cracked kettle on which we beat out tunes for bears to dance to, while all the time we long to move the stars to pity.

God called the light day and the darkness he called night
and brought before Adam every beast, every fowl
for him to name.

                  At Endeavour River, Sidney Parkinson tried
to draw a kangaroo from distant glimpses and dead specimens.
He may not have seen one hop and couldn't get it right, his sketches
show the crossings out, the ghostly re-drawn legs that could, perhaps,
simulate the motion of a greyhound. (He never finished his attempts,
dying in Batavia, renamed Java, of dysentery and malaria).

                                  I try to name myself,
the given name I never use, mother's forgotten maiden name,
the surname I inherited and have already handed on.
I try to name the world - rock, sand, bird - and shape the words
that correspond to you.
I try to call the images
I have inside my head, filter dictionary noise,
but words stick in my throat, or lead to other words
like beads on an endless string. We finger them
successively, wear them smooth, never able to tell
which one came first, which last. They clack together
hollowly like prison doors, like dislocation,
ringing the promise of what is just beyond our reach,
ringing sounds we don't want to hear.

                        If only,
if only, we sigh, looking at midday's clear decisions
in the miraculous dreams of night.

4.

What is the world to me? I shall ask little of it,
I'll let myself float on the current of my heart and my imagination
and if anyone shouts too loudly perhaps l shall turn like Phocion
and say, 'What is that cawing of crows?'

Tired *from going to and fro in the earth and from walking*
up and down in it he stumbles into the river
and pushes against the current, emerging miles upstream
from where he entered.

                        He puts on woollen shoes, drags leaves behind him
and, towards evening, draws spider web across a cave so it looks
undisturbed. He goes deeper,

                        lights fire in the dark, picks up his chains
and dances with the black reflections on the wall.

Invisibility is not enough.

In the morning the web is hung with dew. Currawongs call

and tracks lead back towards the river.

5.
Let us love the muse and love her and love her.
the child that may be born is of minor importance:
the purest pleasure is in the kissing.

I'm caught in those frozen fluid moments of the dive.

I breathe deeply through my nose, arms swing down
then up, knees flex, the commitment of calf and thigh,
and toes abandoned to the springing board.

                                          Eyes wide open
I'm launched into air, exposed and reaching for the apex,
                                                             then the pike
and retardation, dropping with plumbline gravity, fear, some grace,
towards that uncertain reflection and the clouds,

the splash, a consummation or obliteration.

So we keep coming back
                        because we remember
or we hope, climb ladders to the sky, stand poised
as though we had a choice, sensing the distance
between what it is and what it might possibly be,

my apparently solid body given to air, promised to water.

6.

What an awful thing life is, isn't it? It's like soup with lots of hairs floating on the surface. You have to eat it neverthetheless.

Is there a time to give it all away?
                                      I'm trying
to act my age and trying not to act my age, driving
down the Pacific Highway touching one hundred,
a half-moon tilted beside me like a dhow, splashing up just ahead,
sinking behind the clouds.

                        I'm trying to catch my lights,
thinking, inappropriately, of Giles Corey having rocks
piled up on his chest. When his inquisitors ask
if he's had enough, he just replies, 'More weight.'

I'm thinking of witches flying through this night,
and of the seducing incubi and succubi perceived as weight
pressing down upon our sleeping bodies.

I'm locked into my flying car, wrapped in a heavy coat,
driving on the perimeter of this turning earth not sure
whether the wheel is drawing me towards the centre
or flinging me off the edge, not sure whether I'm alone
or that's a kiss on my lips.

Night throws off sparks like stars, draws out tears like rain.

Underfoot

Coleridge careened rock to rock, tripped Hazlitt by his heels,
zig-zagging between ideas, while Wordsworth, on a similar path,

favoured a steadier, measured foot. Even Wallace Stevens
took a break from calculations to walk a poem round the block.

Mandelstam stepped his verse between an exile's walls,
turned and turned again, two metres on, two metres back, the hum

inside his head pulled down to frozen earth, the memory
of those solitary lines climbing into Akhmatova's brain.

The slow walking meditation of the breath,
Jay Ram, Jay Ram, Jay Jay Ram, step after step,

through bamboo stand and scent of rice, past
butcher's shop and factory smells, the mendicant tread

that colonises one foot's span and gives an equal space away,
no lasting imprint of this bi-ped balance on the spinning earth,

on slippery river stone and fields of broken shell,
a pilgrim language in which the going is also coming home.

The HEAD by way of EAR, the HEART by way of BREATH
the eye that feels the pebble in the cushion of the heel,

the instep of a dancer's flight, the electric flash
when mind is earthed like lightning underfoot.

Letter to a Live Poet

for Bruce Beaver

I bought your book of letters twenty years ago
when I was reading Ginsberg, Dransfield, Hall,
McGough ... Just out of university
and teaching up the coast. From a shelf
it oversaw my cribbed and cabined verse.

Reading it now the letters come so new
but then, unread, it was an ornament
of my intent, shameful affectation,
I admit, of sensibility.

Today I walked around Rushcutters Bay,
saw the sea-struck sand and mess of Manly Beach,
tried to work out who those poets were
and how, then and now, you saw inside my head.

Your storm broke at four, mine begins at six,
you ended spitting pips into the morning's maw,
I drizzle on, dripping with Wordsworthian
affirmation, and forget the thing itself.

I laughed that you'd forseen I'd still to write
my dialectics of romantic love;
you must be laughing too, knowing you'd
knocked that kingpin flat in sixty-nine:

It's almost autumn, I'm writing already,
but more than six birds and seven flowers
don't solve the problem of something to say
and the saying, ah, the saying. Poet,

your terrible poise, your balancing words,
stretched on a line of colloquial pain,
chide me to go deeper, not shy from life,
grow up, earn the gift of the living word.

I'll post my letter on this proviso:
that having read you'll toss these lines
into the incinerator out the back
and return to the busyness of ants,
woodlice and the absurdity of men.

any and all means

I stammer, l grope, I look for any and all means possible and imaginable.
                                                  Henry Miller

matins: here's a salt pan sky cracked and patched with cloud

and i'm naked in the middle of the street   no one notices me
standing there like an angel or an alien   feathers stick out
from my shoulder blades / horns bud on my forehead / my thighs
are haunched and hairy   windows open and close like wings to lift
the brick façades of buildings and carry my distortions to the sky

lauds: a seaplane climbs small and insistent as a wasp

another day is breaking in the gutters / wind soughs
like breath across the tops of empty bottles   down on his knees
a drunk stretches for his paper bag as i grope for the dry words
stored up against winter/ the rough-sawn verbs / the peeled bark
of adjectives / thick-trunk nouns   but my lips are pressed in silence
for what can i do about the pronouns i / me / you / you / we

prime: they're flushing out the pub / plainsong runs along the footpath

i sit uncomfortably in the cinema dark behind dilated eyes
real life plays across the screen after the commercials by pearl and dean
and the jump-cut trailers of presque-vu   surroundsound
gives us nowhere else to go but in the mess of voices one clear note
as sharp and arbitrary as the sudden crack of stone   and cliffs explode
with the impulse / well-known to sailors / to jump into the sea: calenture:
craving: cupidity: concupiscence   it doesn't help to understand

terce: peace and war squeeze bronze flanks with their bronze knees

caravaggio is fighting with the shadows / drawing down the dark
to wrap those white limbs / his dagger drawn and plunging in the restless
skimarchy of the mind: the monsters goya set loose in his black sleep
there's an impression that ships of the line are absorbed by turner's
hazy light or they emerge margaret olley has five paintings on the go
bowls of fruit/ the table and the tablecloth / cornflower after cornflower
after   in buckets outside the delicatessen orchids nod like society ladies
over champagne flutes / top-heavy with the elegant colour of their coiffure

sext: there's a froth of rising gulls above the shaken cloth of sea

barbed hopes are weighted to the waves   we believe they're there / translucent
as jelly with black dot eyes / silvered / speckled with gold / hooped
with tiger stripes / the common and the rare   tide turns and still
we bait our hooks and let the line run through our hands hoping
for just one kingie or red emperor / as disciplined as a horsehair bow /
the cruel consideration of scorpion fingers around the violin's neck

nones: the body leaves a pit like a smallpox scar when it steps out to die

i'm thinking thoughts about thoughts and thoughts about sensations
i think i feel but don't understand and emotions i think i've left behind
that keep coming back   i'm concentrating on the road / that wicked
left-hand turn on arden street with no clear view to the right / thinking
about coogee aquarium where the shark coughed up a man's arm
and i used to swim / listening to the radio/ watching the sea dance like tents
randomly pitched and struck in a grey field of scudding light

vespers: below the sky a silver wing / above the sea a white sail

The Distance and the Heat

The river's dried up, just the hard sheen
of mud and the cracks like lizard skin
to tell where water once had pooled

and the smell that rises with the day,
the rotting on the bank, the release
of flies and heat a prelude to the bones.

The sky's a high enamel blue ballooning
from the fixed horizon, the expectation
of morning cloud painted out by noon.

A yard of rusted things — the clapped out
engine block, the plough with broken teeth,
forty-four gallon drums, a water tank,

the low ramshackle of the chicken run,
two black-eyed tractor tyres, children's toys,
twists of wire — the residue of better times.

There's no thought of mending the boundary fence,
no talk of breaking drought, no plans
beyond waiting through the afternoon.

And no relief at night, just dark. The stars
are razor cuts in a tight-stretched cobalt sky:
in bed between us the distance and the heat.

At A Slight Angle

At the intersection of three states
I chase a shadow on the waves,
joined somewhere near the knee.

My feet slice air, sink water holes,
dig in the sand and leave no trace
beyond this skin and after tides.

I run through shifting borders, no will,
no identity or status to declare,
shadow gone before, behind, not there.

Waves break thought to arcs of light,
amber boundaries looping up the beach
dissolve in sea or dry to sand.

Sun strikes me like a wand,
wind turns me like a sail
and I revolve the stillness

of this body's moving moment,
the curvatures of sand and sea,
sliding east, rolling west,

running north and south,
stateless on this tilted edge,
at a slight angle to the world.

Approaching the Edge

Life lies always at some frontier, making sorties into the unknown.
M. C. Richards

1.
What did they suppose, those Age of Discovery mariners,
as they sailed towards the known world's rim?
Were there any atheists on those European ships?
Some knew Pliny had reported tribes whose one leg
doubled as a parasol, men whose nostrils
functioned as a mouth and that the Garamantes
were promiscuous, like sailors. Some heard Iambulus had visited
a 'happy isle' where the inhabitants clicked divided tongues
and spoke two ways at once. Some believed Raphael Nonsenso
sailed to Utopia with Vespucci, unaware the Greek
meant 'no place'. Most, I suspect, had glimpsed cow-hide
and vellum maps, the plated backs of serpents
eating their own tails, the script 'terra incognita'
and ink coastlines that started as approximations
and trailed away into the sea. They may have fancied dragons,
giants, men with horns and wings, women with barking heads,
the wondrous beasts that travellers sighted but never
managed to bring home. There would have been a moment
that they couldn't see, a moment when they could have
drawn back, before their ship felt the tug, the current
above a waterfall, and they were swept towards the edge.
Where did this water go? Where was I about to fall?

2.

It's only from the air that the western desert paintings
make sense to the European eye - dunes in a dry creek bed,
passages between waterholes, the return of Halley's Comet.
Maps and Dreaming. Is it all known and passed on,
a negotiation and representation of the world
telling the lies that get to truth? To what did they aspire?
Does anyone remember Icarus now, or Daedalus,
the greatest inventor of his age? Who made the axe,
the wedge, the wimble, sails for ships and built the labyrinth.
And the son ... such primitive technology, paper and wax,
and ninety-three million miles to the sun. From Stanwell Tops
we float beneath nylon sails, hang from carbon fibre rods,
all the physics calculated to defy gravity for a while.
But there's only one direction so we must land
and carry our contraptions back up the cliff if we're to fly again.
Aldrin, Armstrong, Collins knew where they were going
better than Magellan whose circumnavigation
took twelve days short of three long years. Their maps were clear,
complete, we watched them all the way, a small step, two hundred
and thirty thousand miles and just four days away.
The footprints they left on the moon will last at least
ten million years. Which is more frightening, to know
exactly where you're going or think you'll never know?

3.
Anaximander thought the earth a cylinder suspended
from the vault of heaven and it's been round, rectangular
and oval since. The Mappaemundi depicted earth as flat,
Jerusalem its centre, sea around the clustered land.
There was order in the heavens, astrology unified
terrestial and celestial realms and even thunderstorms
were humours of the gods. A lawful universe:
sailors set their course by the stars, spirits lived in water
and in fire, were placated by rites and sacrifice.
Without auguries, entrails, Newton could predict the future;
on a piece of paper, calculate the past: a lawful universe,
though his rigid laws of motion were another myth. Matter roams
more or less at random, and we are atoms caught between
too many worlds, undecided where to go, energy created
and destroyed. The further Hubble sees the more we shrink,
yet I blink and Jupiter's moons respond. The universe
may be expanding, might be infinite, might not, could be
curved into a hypersphere without a boundary, nowhere
a centre or an edge. Could be doughnut shaped, a labyrinth,
wormholes where we live other lives in a different time
and place, or a Mobius strip so we go round and come back
mirror images of ourselves. There are singularities
from which no traveller has returned. God may not play dice,
but the world's a game of chance and we're high rollers,
shaking our fists, blowing into cupped hands,
murmuring 'seven, seven', shooting snake's eyes.

4.
How very different we are and how alike.
On the edge of Pulpit Rock I lie on my back,
look to the sky locked above me like the hatch
of a bathosphere and descend, the pressure equal
and increasing on either side of its tight skin.
Theoretically, travelling near the speed of light,
we could circumnavigate the galaxy in about four years
and return four hundred thousand years after we set out.
Time does not move but we chase our future into the past
and can't hold on to now. You sit with your legs hanging
into the cold air trapped between banks of cliff. Below you
each tree is clear and distinct; across the valley
they run in waves and intermingle until the canopy
is a plum-blue sea. Mist drifts towards the south-west falls.
Magellan took thirty-seven days to cross the straits
that bear his name, a narrow, twisting passage
through mountains clamped in snow; had already
executed one ship's captain – mutiny – and lost one ship
to storm. Another doubting captain took the San Antonio
back to Spain. Magellan passed from Atlantic to Pacific seas
but how to separate one drop of water from another
undifferentiated drop? We're sailing different seas and similar,
you and I, looking up or down, seeing monsters.

5.
My sails are wanting for the wind. Between their slack canvas
and the water sun repeats and I shade my eyes to look
to the rudder and a rope hanging from the stem.
I look for your figure on the shore, the creaking fixity
of the pier, the sandstone blocks that make the promenade,
the way the grass grows up towards the rotunda balanced
like a fo'c's'le in drydock for repairs. One Empire Day
we built a bonfire in the park, let off Roman Candles, rockets,
Catherine Wheels and threw bungers between each other's legs.
A match fell into one boy's stash and it blew up,
a revelation that left him shocked to tears: in seconds
the merging of a black hole and a neutron star
expels the energy the sun lets go in ten billion years.
When white light strikes the upper atmosphere
it scatters to create blue sky; at the horizon, the pressure
and greater depth of air deplete the shorter frequencies
and we see red though each colour has its shade of grey.
Low tide grounds a fleet of bluebottles, sails swelling
in the sun. Boys burst them with their feet or pick them up
on sticks and chase their sisters up the beach.
After Magellan had been killed, Juan Sebastian del Cano
assumed command. Shipworm forced him to abandon
the Conception, and the leaky Trinidad was left behind.
I look towards the far edge of the sea, the straight line
between a double shade of blue, the tinfoil glints
that spark like uncertainty on a radar screen.
My charts are waterproof, I have a radio, dry food,
spare batteries for the beacon should the boat capsize.
I can find no more words to give you, my lips
the hatchway to a locked sentence, my eyes shut tight.
Still the wind does not come and I make no move.

6.
Where do I end and you begin? What marks the border between us?
We walked from India to Nepal without knowing,
threw away the dope when we turned to see a watchtower
with a flag. Even this was unmanned so, unwilling to go back,
we went on to find the river was up and there was no way
to get to Kathmandu. Indo-Chinese countries wrap around
each other like sleeping bodies, Vietnam folds both Laos
and Cambodia in its embrace. The Berlin Wall
split the world between east and west. Magellan sailed
to see on which side the Spice Isles lay, in Portugal's domain
or Spain's, but there's no fixed point, just directions
and relationships. He left Seville with five ships, two hundred
and seventy men or thereabouts. Del Cano returned
with just one ship and barely twenty men. When I lie by you,
am I touching another or myself, can we be considered separate
when we interact? Did we choose this small bed
or is our existence here some unlikely chance? There's a tendency
to follow a pre-determined path but deviations do occur
and are significant on a sub-atomic scale. The Greeks,
the church, Newton, all were wrong but the world worked for them —
even for Einstein belief's as powerful as truth.
In the beginning was the bang and the end may be one too —
between the first and last frontiers we walk no-man's-land,
look for cow-hide, vellum, the spoor of unicorns, ask for water,
abandon hope, and wake to hope and fail again. On the border
silence stands guard, its edge suspicious as a customs officer's eye,
each word a possible transgression, a clue to a smuggled heart.

Misplaced Heart (2003)

The mind is a small bird hovering
to outface a wind blowing from the sea.
It's hard to find the attention needed
to remain so still, minute realignments

incidental to the long moments
of presumption: a reluctance to evade
or acquiesce. Surely the purpose
must be more than food or procreation.

Mind derives from bird and bird from mind,
thought and thing in tandem more or less.
Wind veers sharply and bird skids sideways,

not hovering now. Mind beats furiously
to find a course, shadows and sunlight
indiscriminately at its wing.

Sunday ·

The rowboat makes its awkward progress
against the ebb, never quite balanced between
the dip and pull of oars. Dragonflies —
mostly grey, almost transparent, more movement
than thing, one with highlights of orange and blue —
skitter from point to point. I put my back into it,
resist the temptation to look over my shoulder,
listen to wood leverage against rowlock
and watch you sitting in the stern, your upturned face,
eyes closed in full sun, your thighs a bric-a-brac
of leaves, your long white toes tipped with mud
and the haphazard water that's washing them clean.

A raven before the dove

It becomes winter overnight, a ministry of grey
translucent rain that defines and obscures.
Reflective invisibility. An unwelcome intimacy
on skin that shivers and goes blue. Surface, touch,

the body meeting weather and turning away.

Rain drives us under and inside, confirms the similarities
between night and day, no shadow when all is shadow.

What I'm reading is full of rain. A tongue bracketed by its mouth
the ear and its propositions, the promises a body makes.

Rain can flatten out but doesn't always calm,
element to element, water on water, water on sand.

Set in motion, water, no matter how big or small the body,
swirls in patterns we can chart, seahorse, conch, cochlea,

the perfect sudden circles of rain falling into pools.

Each wave breaking on the shore imitates
another, each unstable moment of itself, becoming.

Drops of rain, moon, tide, swell, critical mass.

Wind blows surf out or holds it up, no beginning
to the sea, a false conclusion on the beach,
patterns of spilt milk in the lulls. So much coming in

we forget what's streaming out and must swim hard
staying still. That rock doesn't move, weed drifts under us,
sand blooms. Breathe, breathe, panic at the muscles like a knife.

༄

Seagulls are diminished. They feather slick wet wings,
turn heads back against their bodies, facing and not facing rain.

༄

Things weigh more in rain. Even inside, the air is
heavy and slow, an atmosphere of fathoms.
The sky coming in closer and pressing down.

Just when it can't get any louder
it does, so loud you have to imagine
the silences that make sound, the silences
in a house, in a body, in a heart you feel beating
more than you hear. The questions rain asks:

How long can this go on? Will the roof hold?
Why can't we hear each other any more?

༄

What would it have been like inside Noah's oppressive ark?
The fug, the stink, rain falling, water rising, the tense faith,

the (im)possibility of hope, everything two by two
and squashed together. (His wife didn't want to go on board.)

Noah sent out a raven before the dove.

In the car rain swims towards me horizontally,
the windscreen and the mirrors liquefy,
and water lies (in)visibly on bitumen's adhesive skin.

Four times my wheels lock and I slip sideways, uncertain
if I'll regain control. Trucks speed by in the outside lane.

On the radio a Canadian writer says, *Rain,*
'rain' is the most beautiful word and I hear
the words of an old song: *what am I to do, can't help it.*

The mind goes back and forwards. Grey matter.

Rosellas fly their miracle across the road.

Letter while flying

The world's reduced to a cabin window,
now sea-coast, now cloud, now interrupted
sandy tracks under foreshortened trees, and height is
more dislocation than detachment, the uneasy trust
that must be given to technology if we wish to escape
the down below. It's so smooth at 30,000 feet.

I've decided, l mean to tell you, I hate flying too.
It's the take-off, the way the engines tense themselves
and charge, the same and opposite as abandonment
to a wave – there's no contact going up, apart from;
not like going down and into. Flying's a cryogenic state,
straight-line stimulation, the brain cells dropping out
as air filters in. I hope there's more to death than this.

You know the way sparrows flying in formation
suddenly agree to make patterns of their own,
then just as suddenly coalesce as though their many bodies
had a single mind or at least a single purpose?
Perhaps we look like that to birds, distance lending shape
to randomness. No matter how connection
attenuates, originality can only be defined
as degrees of unravelment from the flock.

It's different on a plane, a rigid pattern has been imposed
by need. It's silly to kick against necessity or the
obviousness of thought, the way it flukes and flits.
Billy Wilder had ten rules for making films.
Rules one through nine: don't be boring. Rule ten,
l forget. Where does that leave Beckett,
Proust, big chunks of Joyce or almost

any thought – I'm scared to think of poems, at best
third-rate philosophy, someone said. Writing about
thinking about thinking by writing of something else.

I see no alternative to this trajectory. We'll land,
brakes straining to absorb the re-connection.

*The mind is a tightrope walker balanced
between nowhere and somewhere else.
There must be a way forward but each step
sets the wire swinging and you must pause:*

*the hiatus of a foot raised but not yet
put down, the desire to seem elegantly
in control, the fear that you appear
about to fall, a slipper stretching to hold on,*

*arms feathering a sky that slips
so the earth's spin sets you at an angle*

*stretched inside a blue balloon, like Leonardo's
study of proportions, hands and feet braced on air.*

*It might be distance diminishes
with each step. It might just multiply.*

Let it go (hold on to)

all this immensity / in a measured world
        Marina Tsvetaeva, 'The Poet'

We have no words for the sound waves make.

It seems the sea is crying. 'Lost, lost,' it says,
spilling the words from a big, misshapen mouth,
noise tumbling across all sense, the desperate
ragged hurling against rocks and sand, all that
rolling in and breaking on something solid.
'Nowhere to go, nothing else to do,' it moans.
Green swells rise, topple, turn over on themselves

like something trapped that's been trapped a long time.

We are connected by sound and navigate

acoustically, the changing pitch of the engine's growl
as we step onto the road, the surf we hear
a block away, a voice hesitating on the phone.
Invisible cracks in summer, mosquito drone,
cicada whirr, the pitch and frequency of FM radio,

more than we want to hear, less than we need to know.

Blue whales map their deep world in the time it takes
their voices to go out and come back again,
precise, sightless journeys through mountains
and ravines on songs too low for human ears.

At my feet a mynah with a yellow beak
and robber's mask - a repeated syllable, 'cheep, cheep,'
to hold me up. What can it make of me, big in the world,
striding across the ground with all these words.

༜

We live in light or a variation of its opposite,
the many hues we mix or are mixed in us.
Light picks up words from waves, leaves some behind
in the baffle of leaves. 'What do you make of this?'
each colour says. 'Can you resist this bright sun, this ghost moon
the slick haze on the horizon that might be radiance?'

Clouds stretch, strain, and come apart in gulfs of blue.

༜

We claim things with our words, names like leashes,

not just 'my', 'mine', but ' light', 'sea', lightship, lighthouse,
seahorse, seagull. The sea is not an angry dog or hawthorn hedge.
The cool web of language doesn't wind us in,
it scoops tidal pools, collects tiddlers, weed, jellyfish,
water running through the holes in its taxonomy.

Like a detective I interrogate the signs.
Like Paul Klee I walk through the landscape on a line.

༜

The body remembers what the mind tries

to forget, a glass-frosted winter sea, a kapock sky,
fingers on the spine. The past moves through us
like a torch, like a wave, and in its passing
we drown again and again. So many things
make so little sense, leaving and coming back,
dreams and nightmares, the paths we follow
without knowing we are on a path at all.

I make myself air, stone, water, the intersection of surfaces;
calculate positions, instants, the limits of porosity.
I skip the back of water, the thin air,
diminishing arcs and sudden, slow submergence,
light turning green, darker green, brown,
the adhesion of water's second skin,
the way it accommodates a shape
and lets it go (let it go), the sinking,
a fish that's already forgotten, weed that
makes way, the settling, brown mud rising,
the rich microbial life of silt, the cells at
the heart of stone, the pressure on even a stone

to cohere inside an apparently single skin.

I'm trying to think as a fossil might think,

the moments before and just after time stopped,
the incremental present of limestone's clasp,

the pressure and chemicals that make it work,
this flat imprinted life so different from
the soft embrace of bog. Stone splits and time restarts.
Ammonite, concentric rings like trees,
like shells, the aesthetics and outline of a memory.

What you touch is impermanence, what touches you
lasts longer. Let it go, let it go (hold on).

A rip pushes a rough path through the swells,
it's the easy way out but we're still pulled
here and there and must fight to hold a bearing,
a flagpole on the surfclub roof, a Norfolk Island Pine,
a whitewashed boathouse door. Waves run at right-angles
from the rocks, collide with other waves like traffic
at an unmarked intersection and we can't choose
direction, twisted so our heads and hearts point one way
and our legs are dragged another, waves slice together,
double up and fling us in the air or we flounder in dead water,
wishing for flippers, wishing for feathers or fins.

We think we swim towards the heart, 'No, no,'
the sea shouts against our chests, trying to push us back.

We never leave the perimeter the least expression of its depth.

The immanence of water and transcendence of light,
how far each penetrates - our impression of the former
dependent on the spectrum our eye accepts —

blessed, baptised, enlightened, drowned, struck blind.

The sea's rolled out in bolts of cloth
this night, moonlight puckers the surface
like raw silk. Where light cannot reach
there is a hard black sheen, an edge that
moves but can't be crossed. I lie flat
and listen to the driven waves, feel
the intermittent thud of swell against the cliffs.
I make out rocks, islands that once were
coastline peaks and watch the ocean's tail
flick behind the point, my horizon stretched
between its twin-tipped flukes.

We do only be drowned now and again

'A man who is not afraid of the sea will soon be drowned,' he said, 'for he will be going out on a day he shouldn't. But we do be afraid of the sea, and we do only be drowned now and again.'

J. M. Synge, *The Aran Islands*, 1907

1. Life between

It begins to sprinkle on Bondi Beach. A woman shelters
in a picnic shed, her head gathered in her arms,
a man in a plastic jacket contests the invitation of his line,

flips a silver fish against the rocks, slips a knife along its belly.

Cliffs cut into a stilling sea and sea undercuts the rock,
one limit of the ocean or one measure of the cliff,
the texture of the immaterial and intransigence of things.

One part in air, one part in water, my face swivels
across an intersection, a crack between night and day
as improbable in its opening as its closing, a space
I'm swimming through from wake to sleep to dreams,

edges between a word and what it means on the ear,
water turning coherently to ice, incoherently to steam,
Lear holding the mirror above Cordelia's lips.

I make a brief impression on the sea and pass unnoticed
through the air, skin the border of a country
we call ourselves. Why can't we see our own eyes move?

Aristotle's space was an emptiness between the brink of things.
Now, we suppose, nothing is matter, force,
a mirror of infinity, and where nothing can't be seen
virtual particles are imagined to exist.

In the just-dawn light a container ship becomes
a city, a reef becomes a whale, a plane flying
towards me is as constant as a flickering star,

a resembling that lets us see and stops us seeing
the stone that is a flying fish and the man thinking stone
and flying fish. To reach Serendib you sail for somewhere else
and lose your way, the past subsiding in your wake.

They've taken the mermaid off Ben Buckler Point
where Basso fished for sharks and caught the biggest wave
anyone had seen. Who is able verify this fact?

The rock on which the mermaid sat weighs two hundred tons
and just appeared July, (nineteen-twelve), presumably
tossed up by storm. Around it the shelf fans out
in grazed solidified waves. Its channels make a maze
where one trapped fish swims laps and loose-looped knots.

Seagulls prod, shake and preen, take off and bend against the wind.

In the intertidal zone isopods adapt, carnivorous snails
sneak up on barnacles, sea urchins conceal themselves
in massive hold fasts of kelp while hermit crabs fight
to occupy the most attractive shell. And the rain sets in.

2. Looking down and back

It's a recurring dream. I start to dive under a huge wave
anticipating calm. But I can only bob as though the sea
is supersaturated and I'm a counterbalanced toy

that dips and rocks repeatedly. The wave bears down; I duck my head.

This fear is real – I could drown – and somehow unreasonable.
I keep looking from the beach that narrows to the expanding
seas beyond the point and glimpse reflections in the pit
of hollow waves. What it is to wilfully shut your eyes
against the dark or against the light or see both
and not be able to differentiate. I've seen bodies washed ashore
and struggled to find expression for their faces.

Gulls swing in the freshening breeze; grey sky, grey sea roiling.

Fish change shape and size in the changing winter light
but are still fish. White bellies and silver backs flash.
Under the water my fingers are magnified and strange,
they're polyps or blind pink eels that plead or threaten.

The world is made of metaphor that some call mathematics,
others, expectation; the proximity of two,
a little more than one, a little less than three,
the horizon like a line on a half-full glass.

If we don't act in time, time acts on us, pressing down like a wave.

3. Not knowing where

Moth light on the river. A mist of wings
that run and vibrate. Near night takes them, and streetlights,
lights in windows, the nodding navigation lights

can't bring them back. Three planes dwindle as they track
the river's length. Behind slipping cloud two stars hold
while dinghies bang against the wharf in that silence

which is full of noise. Freeways flex beneath the bridge's
bolted span and glass towers are abstractions
overbuilt against the river's unintentions.

Thick linked chains patrol the levee banks.

I could trace that lean grey-green thread
to its uncertain source or more certain end.
I walk a little way but already know I won't:

trees twisting their roots deeper in the silt,
noises and the mangrove shapes, an unidentified body
fished from tomorrow morning's news.

I wish I'd gone the other way around.

A long autobiography of containment
always getting away from where it was begun,
the second by second inconstancy spoiling at the banks.

I have no convincing name for this,

the leading on to somewhere or to nothing
the standing still not knowing where to go.

4. Staring straight ahead
Rain spits against the windscreen like insect bodies.

The flat land is not so flat, cleared hills rising
moved and masked now by white clouds that,
higher up, swell and thicken, shade to black.

Dead trees stand like stiff hairs on bald hills or, living,
turned black by distance, they are in transit along the ridge.

The dashboard needle swings up, drops down, sweeps an arc
from my left shoulder tip to my right, the way purpose
comes and goes and distance coalesces into time.

Why can't I get a station on the radio?

Three white horses graze aisles of geometrically planted trees.
Black cattle fix their teeth to the ground and sheep are disguised
as clumps of grass, then can't be distinguished from the rocks.

Sometimes the sky blows up like a giant balloon.
Sometimes it's curved and close like a contact lens.

Weather surrounds the car and closes in.
Looking back I can't see beyond the window and, in front,
wipers separate the rain like blades slashing through wet reeds.
There's a new cold in my shoes and underneath my jeans

and a hint of rainbow trying to supplant the clouds.

Things are strung together or forced apart:
looping telephone lines, barbed wire stretched
from pickets or split wood, trees that line the road
shaking and shaped by wind. The highway is direction,
towns intention — no lines next 10k, Leeton
53 Narrandera 81— and speed the means.

A flock of birds billows above a stranded tree,
storks rise from below a bridge, drop and stretch
their long white necks. What moved them to move
to where it may be better, may be worse?
Low to the ground sparrows scoot like dust
(you don't know who I am; I'm not prepared to say).

The road is turning away towards the sky,

above me cloud opens as a blowhole does
in rock. Instead of water spurting up
light streams down and is impossible to ignore.

The mind is a body breathing in unconsciously
and consciously breathing out, an imperceptible
pause between the operations, coming near to full
and just as near to empty, always something

left behind or a space to fill, dying a little
and being born again, the warm exhalation
like gently beating wings passing from a cloud,
cooler, fine-grained wind entering like a ghost:

an interchange between the starry skies above
and the moral law within, *words assembling*
as if they might be things in-and-of themselves,

while a ceiling fan revolves above two sweating,
naked figures in a cheap hotel, and entwined zephyrs
blow Botticelli's Venus *across a choppy sea.*

The mind is a kind of theatre *and we
are actors and audience successively
and simultaneously in the dark
or spotlit and near blind.* Thoughts pass, re-pass,

glide away and mingle *beaked and masked
as birds,* metaphors, metonyms and anthropo-
morphisms, *like need, desire, intention, purpose,
simplicities of cause and effect. We have no notion*

*where the act takes place: initials scrawled on orders,
siren threads in the leaf-scratch, rain-dance night.*

*Catastrophe is scripted as recursion:
a moon scooped out by shells is mode-locked*

*on the earth, we see its many phases but just
one face, plausible dust curtailing resolution.*

Aubade and evensong: new year, 2003

The sun rises like an orphaned, bloodshot eye.
Drain pipes are stuffed with tennis balls, residents stand on roofs
and drizzle water down the walls. Sheep catch fire,
the telescopes at Mount Stromlo fuse and I see a holy city
coming out of heaven as a bride adorned and hear a great voice

warning us to be alert but not alarmed.

In Nauru, Iraqi refugees throw stones at their custodians. How long,
how long, one man asks, not realising
he's been excised from time. At Wattamolla two freckled girls
defy signs to leap from the highest rock,
gingerly an Indian man jumps waves, and pelicans on the lagoon
glide with the dignity of dowagers at a ball.
Meanwhile, in Patagonia, a blue macaw, the last one in the wild

mates with a related species.

At the Pool of Remembrance the sun makes compromises
to splash the earth in dominoes.
Around them pigeons waddle, ibis graze, lovers stretch belly
to belly in the grass and shadows are
the ghosts of Hiroshima, the naked, napalmed girl
running down the tarmac in Vietnam.

Backpackers lie on Coogee Beach in the smell of their own basting.

As clouds mass above McKenzie's Point, boys fling themselves
to the wet dark space pressed flat
by the weight of sky, ignoring or oblivious to the properties
of water. They float like stars,

beat tight sea-skin with their hands, kick navel-high and shout
for the blue-black emptiness, the expectation,
the fat drops of rain, that lightning sheets cloud to cloud or plunges
over there over here. Counting five seconds to a mile

they run back up the beach. Light crystallises at their feet.

Hump-headed parrot fish consume rock and coral indiscriminately
buck-teeth closing like garage doors.
Beyond the reef the skeleton of a cathedral or a carousel
rises to the gathering dark.
From its rotating outer rim sex and death are ringing bells
and beating drums to compete for our attention.

Clowns disport from metal wings in disciplined abandonment.

In Manhattan they can't find a dove to commemorate 9/11.
To make do, they buy squab. Weak-winged fledglings, they cannot fly
and smack, instead, into plate glass or plummet
to the Hudson River. One perches on a wire and will not move.
The Prime Minister stands on tiptoe at the cabinet mirror applying
appropriate expressions. Material breach, he tries. No commitment
he pipes, then drops an octave: There is no ambiguity in our desire
to rid the world of terror. He checks an upright mirror at his back.
The president sits up in bed, pops a Coke, and promptly
falls asleep. On his lap a copy of Sun Tzu. The television crackles,

his eyelids twitch

a host of angels falling, a reign of fire.

Prequel : Sequel

to write the moment as a simile bodies falling from the sky like mutton birds

to write fire black cloud white cloud dust sirens screams sobs wailing the silence that ghosts each sound; flags and photographs unconfirmed reports unnamed officers unidentified sources   victims suspects culprits; to write 'good will triumph over evil'

to write a jellyfish inside a rabbit so it glows a fish inside a tomato so it lasts; intelligent slime that negotiates its way around a maze rat-like but not like a rat; a mouse with a human ear on its back; to stop light in a laboratory and play with it a little; to write that even earthworms show a tendency to integrate

to keep your eyes closed give no indication roll away; to lie as if if you could you'd be anywhere else as if you've gone away and left a coffin in your place; say something talk to me; (keep quiet please don't say anything please don't touch me)

to remember a word like charabanc or omnibus or rickshaw or tank; wheels turning tracked and trackless; the shoed and shoeless padding boulevardes stones twigs grass mines; to mediate horizons behind fat-tailed sheep and border guards leaking scows and flying fish proclaiming sand on bondi beach

no more plump pigeons slithering snakes or flaming suns; no more refractory mules no sapphire waters; no taxidermy of ideas savage bodies unearthed skulls

to write 'we start from any point and arrive at the sublime'.

Commentary: two days

> *Over all the face of the earth*
> *Main ocean flow'd, not idle but with warm*
> *Prolific humor sof'tning all her globe*
> *Paradise Lost*, Book VII

On the thirteenth day a Shi'ite holy city is a speed bump before Baghdad;
still the people don't comprehend we intend to make them free.

All Fools Day, the first day of the cruellest month, and here too
things are poised. Easter's gone or coming; the sea, at Bronte,

is warmer than the air, politicians lie indignantly and Persephone,
who fills her lap with daffodils, is raped by Pluto. Her mother

seeks the echo of a scream and blocks the harvest of the world.
It is cruel. Wherever I go, Gilgamesh cries, wherever I look,

there stands death. Hammurabi promises to slay any man
who turmels into another man's mud hut. He begs the oppressed

come before him as a righteous king but Marsh Arabs remember
the first time they were enticed — the apricot, the snake — and wonder

how they should respond. A Sumerian poet cries, *O Ur,*
like an innocent goat thy kid has perished. On day fourteen

the news is much the same. Scheherazade has been detained,
Sinbad has survived this version of his tale. At the Museum of Modern Art

Zhu Ming floats naked on the harbour in a plastic bubble, sharks
are radar-guided, sea-anemones might be hand grenades,

and I lie inside a four-channel, seven-video projection
on a 360° fabric screen, as all around me water bubbles,

falls and then, in an optical illusion, rises up again.

*The mind is the surface of a pond expanding
predictably from where the pebbles struck,
unpredictably bouncing back, each intersection
an independent universe that lawfully configures*

*three rosellas and the diagram of an autumn tree
into textures that are neither bird nor branch,
as if, in the act of falling, transparency obscured
as much as it let in, a seeming that is not*

*motionless. Even the pebbles, apparently still and fixed
in the mud. What we think is not always what we see:
we're like Vesalius dissecting corpses from the scaffold,*

*dividing a hand from the wrist, wrenching an arm
fron its shoulderblade, disconnecting legs at the knee,
unaware a black-finned shark might be a coloured bird.*

For a child

First there is silence
pressing round like you imagine
the atmospheres of depth.

Then the old words
we have cheapened or forgotten
like terrible, everlasting, lamentation.

Then shovelfuls of clay
that strike the coffin as though
the box were hollow,

hoes rising and falling,
and a baby crying and crying
though her mother bends

to give her milk.

For my brother and sister

It's the movement of the wind, the movement
of leaves way above you and the unkempt grass
against your shins, the ragged hiss
and sssh moving in and out of silence

that blurs discrimination between dead
and alive a cemetery might be thought
to signify. It's what exists between the graves,
what's missing rather than what remains.

My mother has no gravestone, no sod or plaque
to prove she lived and died. Some documents,
photographs that blush in keeping with the times,
and the three of us to imagine how she was.

(She sets a blanket on the sand and shades her eyes
to watch us swimming, skylarking on the edge —
do you remember if she smiled? — and, sometimes,
we glance up to check that she's still there).

In St Stephens Churchyard light keeps drifting
through the trees but gradually the shadows
interleave a sense that something must be there,
the belief that nothing is beyond this wind.

And asked her how she was

i.m. Sylvia Jean Dixon

There's an irregular drip from the something
frozen plasma — a purple patch obscures
the first word — the saline, the 5% of glucose
and 9% of something else.

                        They're taking out the lines.

Plastic bags, outlet valves like teats, revolve
whether from a breeze that's made its way
to intensive care or from our movements
round the bed. A needle's taped below the skin
but nothing's going in.

                        This morning I said hello

and asked her how she was. There's still a mask
to help her breathe, it's not laboured, almost silent
and we watch her chest rise, the collarbones
above the sheet and gown.

                        She's still with us, looks up,

smiles when the baby smiles, says I love you too,
but prefers, or has to keep her eyelids closed.

She knows it's coming and wonders if it's near.

She hopes for a wooden cottage, a clydesdale,
to be with Alan once again — there's an indentation

where her wedding ring has been removed — and worries
she may have asked too much.

                                            White lines advance
across the bedside screen and coloured numbers pulse —
ninety over fifty, forty-five — but nothing beeps
and no one writes the observations down.

Does death come in or leave, hold on or let go?

It's taking time. There's a frosting on her lips.
Veins have broken on both cheeks, her mottled foreams
are the camouflage of fish that could be swimming
beneath the weed.

                                   It's harder now. She gulps for air and
there's a gasp when she exhales. There's still
a little life, a private, remembered, hoped for life.

She can't answer now. They've turned the screen to grey
but Granny's doing fine, looking back and forward, going home.

Final belief

must be in a fiction
        Wallace Stevens

To pass the time, or for other, hidden reasons,
Melville tells us, sailors practised scrimshaw,
meticulously scraping out the captured bone
to put a trace back in, perhaps the outline of a walrus

or a scene from home. There are artists who include
almost everything, and others who take it all away,
as if the looming might exist in what is yet to come
or what's already gone, as if a voice

could rise from an unexamined text, an embryo
or skeleton, the sayable and what must be left
unsaid, the suggestion of a tadpole's tail,
a veil, a hat without a head, empty shoes

standing at a wall, footprints twice the size of mine
crossing half the beach, fragments that work like art
where, up close, you see the intentions of the palette knife,
the underdrawing, the vermilion in a field of sand.

There's more than just aesthetic difference
between the instamatic image prospectively installed
and the slow permutations of the daguerreotype,
time making space in a different way, a changeling

getting used to transformation. Somewhere,
in the expanse of blue, there's the lamentation
of a great white whale, a demented captain
with a wooden leg, and the spoor of an imagined beast.

The mind is a misplaced heart lopsidedly
beating without shape or sound —
systole — and discordantly — diastole —
navigating chambers of enclosed space:

for fear Mandini de Luzzi refused
to open up the head; Copernicus
restrained the flight of supposition
until he died. The mind

is a metonymic heart enabling
reasons reason cannot know, *it*
makes its way feelingly, negotiating

an emptiness awash with solar wind
and anti-matter, the pulse of unrecorded stars
resolving where absence was presumed.

Postscript : like Picasso

A man's just sitting there on the crescent
taking it all in or letting it all pass by,
the traffic, birdcall, the sun that falls
on his bald head polishing it like Picasso's,
all brown and round and shining,
sitting there like a stone or a frog or a buddha.

He is of it all, even this speeding past,
the wheels that push away contradictions
between the need to grip and the need to
slip away. He must feel the cars pull air after them
in packets, swoosh, swoosh, and another
swoosh, as he sits there in the gaps, persistently.

Uncommon Light (2007)

... spring is still spring. The atom bombs are piling up in the factories, the police are prowling through the cities, the lies are streaming from the loudspeakers, but the earth is still going around the sun and neither the dictators nor the bureaucrats, deeply as they disapprove of the process, are able to prevent it.

George Orwell, 'Some Thoughts on the Common Toad', 1946

Spring

Sun is our measure. The warmth of light between
the elastic bob of leaves. Birds perched on twigs
or seaming blue sky before and after, their sharp cries
existing when they may not, our skin taking in time

and little by little, letting it show. Sunspots.
Keratosis. Our darker selves in and out of seasons.
Leaves put back in array, the sudden mutability
of new growth subordinate to a trunk. So much time
we spend in dreams, disavowals. The war takes,

oh, sixteen days. The war goes on. The tyrant flits
from hideaway to hideaway his face evolving into
a full dark beard: a soldier shoots the Bengal tiger
he once fed between the bars; under the gunfire,
in cafes and in corridors, we minute the becoming order.

Trees are imprinted in the intervening,
a flickerbook of intersections in relation to.
I swoop past here. They sway, the one wind blowing,
always some leaves falling from the mass.

Very like a whale

                        I seem to wake
            and sleep ambiguously,
to see and misconceive,
        to feel on the brink of something
                that doesn't end, beauty
                that is more than beautiful,
                meaning that is more.

The present is all around me, dreams,
        a panoply of crimes, smudges of erasure,
        memory made of clouds, camels,
                weasels and the unlikelihood
        of somewhere within and beyond this world.

Here's light,
        angular, ubiquituous
                with the milky pigments of belief.
Here's plodding time, breathing hard.
                Birds fly up, perch on branches,
        peck seed from the grass, (tug worms from the soil).
        I am not what I imagined,
                here I am the illusionist
                and dupe of my illusions,
        making the angels disappear, wishing them back again.

Stories that shifted in the telling
                    once were true:
                    a virgin birth, a resurrection,
a tiger who regained his human form, a crocodile
who didn't. I'm pitching words against the sea,
              it drags them out,
                flings them back again
still freighted with my weight. The waves are red
                            with blood,

brown with shit, yellow with the sickly light, anything
                    but blue and green.
      I am an insistent fizz and drone,
              deft, adroit, as elastic
              as necessity and chance,

            one more clay figurine with beseeching hollows
            where the eyes should be,
            as different from the others
as I am the same, no more evolved
              than a roach,
              no better than a rat,
              happy as a labrador in the sun.
      This is grace, the rest is commentary
      and I would let it go: in millennia

I'll chatter metaphysics with a chimpanzee, now
            my thoughts are the antlers of the Irish elk,
              the wings of flightless birds, peptides
              spelling out the phrase
              very like a whale. Most organisms

      produce more offspring than can possibly survive.
            Nothing can follow that.
            Something will. Blunt heads of rain,
                    faithless wind,
                        the stricken sun at dusk,

knock-kneed girls somersaulting on the beach,
                  the commonplace surprise
                  of making love face to face,
        the heart breaking apart, an instrumental eye
                      and instrumental mind rejoicing,
                            a last cacophony of birds.

Morning : thinking of you

Outside the wind is at its work.
I can see and faintly hear the pines
flex back and forth irregularly.
From behind the window it seems
a connection and a disconnection.
I think I like the distance — me in here,
the trees out there — it gives the world
its otherness, its fine inhuman dignity.
Momentarily it unmakes me: strange,
inconsistent meditation. Autumn sun
glistens on a sea that is almost flat.
Waves emerge only at the edge
where wind strips spray from rims
and dissipates it like exhaled breath.

Finches perhaps

Birds strip the hanging air, cut through it
between bars, through chinks, always at this

flit-flitting peak, this in and away as we say,
monstrous; as we say, how could anyone

have endured; thinking they, thinking if I were,
as birds dart in micro-moments through

our scant attention to how time corrodes
between denials then and now. It happened

and happened, normal really how helpless
rectify appears. Mind that thinks manacle

and bird and time cants to be a shrug. Tomorrow
the new tyrant's found in a spider hole, he has

a thick white web of beard, he has a gun
he doesn't fire. A torch shines in his open mouth,

the talk again of supervised elections. Distinctions
are this stark: Tuol Sleng – the poisoned mound –

used to be a school; its commandant
taught mathematics; its guards were adolescent.

Coherence only in the birds, what they have re-claimed.

Monster

Before I formed you in the womb, I knew you

in my smallest self, origin as if from nothing,
each successive moment, that which would
be cause, that which would be consequence.

In the unrelenting dawn, I am a perfect silhouette:
I ride with the Janjaweed, I run with the Tonton Macoutes,
I am a Hutu genocidaire; I drive in the gleaming motorcade,
cast my omniscient eye aside.

This is what the monster says:
You are the head of the snake for me.
I am regretful that you didn't die.

Imaginable things and helpless people: they cut off his cock,
stuffed it in his mouth and nailed him to a tree: go,
spread the word: five men held her down and raped her
time and time again; one man used a stick: go,
perpetuate the human race.

This is what the monster says:
I was following orders. I am protected
by the principle of Acts of State. I had to obey my flag.

Shabby armies in their uniform ideas,
beliefs that grease the conscience. Beneath the cap,
I wear the mask, I nurture scars. I am the Banished Couple,

Fallen Angel, Golden Child, playground bully. Each two-bit Freud
has another unconvincing explanation, each bleeding heart
a bucketful of sympathy.

    I am essence coeval with existence,

a monument of steamrolled bones. Uncle Joe, Papa Doc,
Little Boy, Leviathan, Behemoth, Beelzebub, the footprint of some god.

Trepan my skull, count lesions and the dead, the reign of beasts
has yet to end; each generation throws a monster up the charts.

This also has been said:
> *Our grief has turned to anger, the war on terror is well begun.*
> *We go forward to defend the just and good.*

A dark sun rises. A fragment of the moon dissolving like a ghost
lingers in the other sky. Uncommon light sheds little understanding,
what is manifest leaves little room for hope.

Sunday: '(Everything can be) transformed,
deformed (and) obliterated (by light)'
Man Ray

Now light won't be still but glissades down the sky
glints fish scales on water that would be grey.
A cormorant is one black speck on this sharp sea. It dives

where we imagine it darker still though it may be
silvered with the rhythm of small fish. Needing air,
needing to be underwater, if it maintains a straight line, it

should emerge over there, or there. We reach into ourselves
but can't say anything except quite or just,
shaping fish that squeeze through our palms and slip away.

Speech has been selected, the philosopher muses
to out-think thought. He could say an oracle
is just as true when false. This also

a new reality on the ground as is a Man Ray photograph
of a cork, a feather and a spiral object entitled
'Origin of the Species', or the rayographs he invented

in a darkroom accident. Everything conspires, everything
is yoked by restless approximations so anything
may not be one thing or another but both,

a body and its ghost, empty space, dark force. It's hard to know
what's provisional, what eternal, or if the ideas themselves
are to blame, like trying to believe the universe

originates from a single spot or the beaks of finches
are proved fact and consequence. That black butterfly
on the moonflower vine is bigger than the heart-shaped leaves.

It has a blind white eye on either wing. Perhaps we will adapt.

ৎ

Leaf-lie is polarised a rich sienna red, greens are deepened
and I step into my rag-limbed slouch of shadow,
eyeful of thought until a bough cracks my head.

Sea eagles swing above and coming in low and chevron-shaped
is a three-gull flight. A fishing boat drifts above its double,
wheelhouse glimmers skip and are absorbed, distance

in this bird-path, light-path, the vertiginous impulse.
It's as though the sea could suck you down to where
John Foster Dulles says to Nehru, 'Are you with us

or against us,' and he replies, 'Yes.' It's only a matter of time.

ৎ

Thick fog re-shapes Sydney. Sea and sky elide so cliffs
exist as premonition. Cars prowl like cats at night,
the world not quite awake, not quite sure

what will emerge. The new liberators
are caught on film dissimulating sex,
linking hooded men to faux-electric wires.

Comprehension is in the slippage,
the crack between what we think and what
it may turn out to mean. Here hope is weight deferred.

It rankles to think relative in this suspected light.

That beat against the cage

All our stories are commonplace. Seven master plots,
a thread running through them. The quest
we choose or is thrust upon us or, unknowingly,
we pursue, the misunderstanding, missed opportunity,
the offer that was declined for good reason
at the time, the journey to the underworld.

Life lopes away as we dally in sub-plot, or worse
in a stream of consciousness; these thoughts,
sometimes like chirping birds, more often
like the incidental murmur of the sea, or wind
that gusts down evening streets. They never stop.

I'm walking on an inclement afternoon. To my left
the sea is grey and choppy, one swimmer barely visible
among its peaks and troughs. People hunch on the sand
and hug their knees, caught between a wish
and indecision, between things we see as causes
and the consequences that surface in another time.
Thoughts slip in and out of focus, are phantoms,
huckster's patter, intimate and far removed.

The world takes on an intricate, delinquent vagueness
like dust around a planet. The further that I penetrate
the denser it becomes, though the core may be

little more than bafflement: a flurry of white butterflies
that rise and fall, hover momentarily but,
beautiful and mesmerising as they are, never settle.

This is attachment to ephemera, to what is
not fast, not verifiable; to the inconsequential
which seem equations of possibility,
radar screens that illuminate the yet unseen.

It cannot last. Depiction of what pertains
must be plausible. Those moving leaves are wind;
that shadow, spilling wind and leaves
and intermittent light; and there, sharply now,
a wagtail interweaves the shadowlight.

Yet there is confinement when all is in its place,
the mind becomes eye's slave, scribe of boundaries,
reporter of coherence. Is the literal really so?
I think it is. I think it isn't. That clustered about the real
is a different kind of life, a banishment
of stark and solid, not light that bounces off the water
obliterating all in its even-ing glare but mist
with its hazy indistinctions, its bewilderments.

Where is this story leading? To be like or as,
to distinction and concordance, telling all that is,
denying all that seems. The world holds back
a secret for itself, puts up a lattice work

of truth and lies. In the constrained sway of branches
we predict where leaves were, are going, will be
and the paths between, a coming-into-being
in this perception, not the repose of knowledge, only thinking:
within the mouth, the resonance we hear in *hummm*,
within the skull, wings that beat against the cage.

༓

I would see the outline of the world sufficient
had there not been an unconcealment,
as though the wind were taking off its clothes,
a folding and unfolding of bird and tree and light
all the time back to swirling fire, emergent seas.

It's as if I'm deep inside the world, gripped
and almost capable of understanding
the mystery that is no mystery, that yields
but in yielding withdraws behind the clouds.

This seems an alias of beautiful, an inkling
that is in the moment but escapes the present.
Nothing here's sublime, nothing fixed and final,
nothing artful: this records confusion and the mind's existence.

༓

The physical becomes more than physical, the complex whole
thinks freely, thinks it thinks though the parts
are bound. I think these thoughts, I don't think
they think me though they approach as figures
walking down the street. When I reach out

to grasp expected hands they blur, assume my shape
yet don't cohere. They filter through me, separate,
and shimmer in all directions. I sense in these moments
a loss of time, that there has been a passing
which leaves me stranded in an afterimage
of thoughts that pulse erratically. Deliberately,
I see myself as undivided and unconsciously
split again, confusing landmarks and discerning
one solipsistic star amid the muddle of the Milky Way.

It's untenable, this drifting that sees the world as drift.
The fantasy should ebb, become the half-recalled
calling of the sea, or else lifetimes will be spent meandering
self-consciously through the matter of the day,
shuttling back and forth as if transience
could be a domicile, fearful that to stray too far,
stay too long, is to exchange the story
for an understory, the agreed accepted world
for a thesis of perplexity; a conclusion there is
no evidence to decide, or that the evidence
leads to thoughts the thought cannot sustain.

'Am I really the person who bears my name?'

1. This confusion

Daylight saving has begun. It is the soft dark
and the birds have started, especially the one,
he doesn't know which one, that trills just like
a yapping dog. This confusion, the man thinks,
as he lies with his eyes half-shut, is important:
it means attention. He doesn't want to know,
likes the mystery of the bird-dog. Soon alarms
will intercede, the bird-dog disappear.
When it is fully light he will get up but,
for the moment, he enjoys this in-between.
Butcher-bird, bower-bird, bird-man-of-Alcatraz,
he muses. How many names have I been given
and how much information have they conveyed?

2. The mystery of it

The man is sipping coffee in Victoria Street. He is alone
and likes the feel of it, as if he has stepped aside.
He reads the sports pages and the inconsequence
of what he reads is pleasure though he thinks
I have read this all before. There is wind enough
to make the paper awkward. At a table to his left
a young woman smokes and scrunches up
her eyes. He has to choose whether to listen
to her conversation, to become that much a part
of her and her companion's lives, or whether to
disapprove their existence. He has this power and
when he chooses to exercise it, to participate or not,
nothing will change, nothing will be quite the same.

3. That much a part

He trains himself to attend the incidental,
give to trifles the distinction they deserve.
To rain, and the people hunching through it
under black umbrellas to reach the other side,
to seagulls furled in wings on the grass.
Each is wanting shelter, one of place, one of time.
It will pass. As will the different weights of footfall
on dry and soaking earth, and children's laughter
as they stomp in puddles coming home from school.
The man wonders about the raindrops he has carried
along the fine hairs of his arm and that they are
no longer there. I've become romantic, he laughs,
thinking he has not and knowing he wants more.

4. Wanting more

The man can't help making day trips to the future
or the past. I don't want to, he thinks, there's no point,
it only makes me happy or sad and I always
feel out of date. It's like designing and re-designing
a humane zoo so not even the tiger is aware
there is a cage and pads a wilderness narcotic
with the danger of becoming, the cruelty of hope.
This is self-absorption, he murmurs, rootlessness
contingent on the world but without a sense of place.
Bewildered to be just where he is, the man
says moderation and compromise and also
what it is reasonable to expect
but the words taste like paper on his tongue.

5. Just where he is

The neon sign below the awning says 'Heart Queen
Cleopatra Pleasure Paradise Dome of the South'
but the stairwell's jumbled, shadowy, as if
there is an undecided clash of wills. It's easy,
he thinks, to mistake something for what it's not,
to live with misperception until it's real —
a light could be a sign; voice, a proof —
as irresistible as stepping from the pavement
and up the stairs. Having gone up will he come back?
If he does, will he be a man affirmed or,
amazed to be walking twice into the morning,
a man shot through with what he doesn't
understand. He pauses. Steps quickly on his way.

Monster

It's possible I misconstrued you,

laid too much emphasis on the uniqueness of a birth,
failed to acknowledge circumstance could corrupt, sustain;
I indulged myself in accusations against an absolute.

I don't believe what I then believed. You are not responsible

for Leibniz or the Lisbon quake, for the twenty-six-eyed
and sixty-arsed box jellyfish, that the cosmos
is shaped like a soccer ball; or for the dosido
of right and wrong around the garden bed.

You are not the monster I thought you were,

not by definition or necessity the one immutable.
You are a creator caught in a creator's net, in fact
a creature. Every horror has its own pathology,

the disease infects the flock. Prey present as predators,
the malefactors replicate even as the angels
experiment with cures. Each encounter pulls against reductive story,
says I will not, I am just (an instant, an instance),

and reference skews on maps not drawn to scale.

I know saintliness exists. It's all around me.
My next door neighbours in their simple modesty,
the lady down the street who is always

helping someone older than herself. Even the slow
judicial process conceives it natural to be better
than we are. I'm trying to shoo the gloomy birds away

but crows repeat about me on the lawn; and the vulture
and the kite, the cuckoo and the owl: should I have *given up the ghost
when I was drawn from the womb?*

Against immortality

One moment it's as if
a flight of dragons had descended
to seize the temple in their talons

only to find themselves for centuries
likewise clutched and, like the tree roots
and Ta Prohm itself, straining

towards both earth and sky, and then
we're smiling in every second doorway,
in every other frame. And it's when,

scrambling like awkward gibbons up,
multitudes, the halt among the healthy,
swarm the slopes of Phnom Bakheng

to see the sun that sets like this
each day of all our lives, and then,
moments later, cameras round our necks,

we scramble to leave the dark behind.
A blackbird lands on the western wall
of Angkor Wat becoming the highest point

against the dipping sun, so still
it could be statuary. On a gallery wall
gods and demons churn the Sea of Milk,

their tug-o-war to extract the essence
of immortality upturns turtles, fish,
and leaves us – tired, dusty – stuck between.

Tourism : what the I sees

Geckos stake-out restaurant walls. Swelter
      and the crackle of time adjusting gears. Where you from? Where you go?

Hubbub starts at four-fifteen. Delight in this startling,
      what there is to do. I am passive and alert.

Pinch-eyed in the sun cyclo drivers perch
      or pedal for what's passed or yet to come: the present tense.

Space drives by in squares. I gawp
      and see through myself: a bullock in a lily pond.

Motorbike retorts discontinue into rain. Mimosa leaves
      contract when touched. It takes a while to re-connect.

Too much here is out of date. How do we crop time?
      The closer we converge the more evident my detachment.

Boredom locks me in the Presidential Palace. Conversation
    limps into a cul de sac. A lithe brown river swims between the rooms.

We eat duck in citronella by the Perfumed River.
    Boats dredge silt and I answer to Smith or Jones.

Girls cycle by: a school of pedal-winged fish,
    white flowers in their hair: what will it take to shift you?

Bougainvillea bloom as dragon's scales, cockerels squabble
        beside a Mercedes tyre. I'm okay with subjects,
            predicates are hard.

The importance of clouds in unsentimental light.
    The intricacies of each eye, little suns themselves.

Everything alludes to something else. I am circumspect.
    Attentive. Connections topple towards profundity.

Monsoon rain falls as it were a solid thing;
      particle by particle it evaporates as an act of faith.

Incomprehension spikes the waves: if we stand outside the sea
    who knows what goes on for fish.

Now we are translated. The fish are talking bird.
    Here's cogency. Here's the edge. It cannot be other.

Consciousness is not the point, must be the point:
    the ear and eye play ring-a-rosie: we all align.

Enchantment in the pulse between formation
    and some sort of stop: desire endures, is like a halo.

A bird turns suddenly turquoise, turns
    drab again and disappears. Fingers point. The eye insists,

tracks detail longer than expected. Bellying the current
    a rowboat becomes a bird — lapwing, lapwing, lapwing —
        turtles, unicorn, phoenix ascend into capacious night.

Uncommon Light

Dark glasses are the wrong response.

I risk my eyes for sunrise: matter-of-fact.

One world in the corner of my eye; another in my face.

Were my eyes as big as footballs I would look inside the cave.

Arthropoda: crustacean with ancestral eyes: father, mother.

Oddball Nautilus: pinhole camera in a shell.

Consider the perks of camouflage and conspicuousness.

An Atlas moth may be a snake; a moray eel a rock.

White gull, sooty tern: the parrot makes outrageous claims.

A flickering sign: THIS WAY, THIS WAY: I can't make up my mind.

How does a chameleon? Implication breaches thresholds.

The eye: complication and extreme perfection.

An edge we share: it makes conspirators of us all.

Fish eye, owl eye, squint eye, cat's eye, wall eye!

I chase after the light: it tips me first.

Dung beetles roll the sun around my toes.

I say transcendent: love the sky in atmospheric terms.

Starlight becomes us: no, really, divinity adapts as it descends.

Particles of light in the belly of the world.

I choose to direct my eye's attention: sunlight disagrees.

Makes a neat impression: here I am in black and white.

What would you see with second sight? Isn't one enough?

My eyes are laser-made: opacity is challenged: no revelation.

When you say blue, do you mean this blue?

Anyhow, what is light in the light of time?

Predation: digesting what the eye selects.

Angelfish tilt mirrored bodies, thrust and parry shafts of light.

This is all there is, light is not emitted from my eyes.

The eye of self-consciousness is lonely now. Where to hide?

The sensible world may be more than meets the eye: let's see.

Light calls to silence in ecstatic whispers. Listen.

The peacock flicks his tail: doubles his distinction.

This day is my accomplice: I render light: I quiver.

Material but substanceless, the light embodies you.

Turns the sea into a discotheque: dance with me.

The blink of an eye. And you are gone.

Common and uncommon light: who patrols the border?

I forget to watch the sunrise. It rises anyhow.

Thirty-six views of Bondi Beach

In the hollow of a wave
    sunlight, spray, a freckled skipping boy.

He streaks beneath the crest, attentive
    to the glimmering ride; oblivious.

Down the belly of fat north-eastern swells
    he's leaping like a bouncing bomb, against the sea, through the air.

Like fish in a contracting net, lifesavers
    churn the ocean to a frenzy; seagulls screech on angel wings.

She pirouettes as Baz MacDonald sprays oil
    on skin as rich as amber. Umbrellas, igloos, tans for hire.

Louis the Fly slaps hamburger on the griddle, hops, bristles, scowls;
    fat plops and spits at Greasy Mick's

Straight-backed as Cleopatra's Needle the stink-pipe crowns the cliff;
    cleated fishermen cast for blackfish in the murk.

4pm. Billy Jenkins sea-sways from his car, skips rope,
    gives the heavy bag a fearful whacking. 'piss today, piss today'.

The Rex Hotel. 10pm. Cyril turns his spectacles upside down,
    bites bums, sings, 'we gotta get outta this place'.
    Bouncers help him on his way.

༃

In the hollow of a wave
    the wink of an eye, the slingshot moment.

A surfboat slews, stalls, digs in by the bow,
    catapults the sweep and oarsmen through the air.

Underwater, a parachutist tosses and tangles in his sheets,
    three men swim him to the surface, can't bring him back to life.

The Whale taps his Christmas morning keg: let us beach bums
all be jolly, fleck the sand with sunburned folly.

Bed legs paddle in jam jars full of kerosene:
   Cairo Mansions: top floor cockroach disincentives.

Doogsa Davis: if I catch you two cunts again
   I'll crack yer fuckin' knees across the gutter.

Surreptitiously, lanky boys and barrel-chested men
   check out the tits on display beside the promenade.

Aub Laidlaw escorts a too-brief bikini from the beach,
   catches one of his inspectors cavorting with a topless girl.

He leans on the face of the sun's last wave,
   slips, flips, rolls like a carpet up the sand,
      runs barefoot to catch a 380 home for tea.

In the hollow of a wave
    an enfolding, unfolding like a fan.

Bug-eyed sun, gem-bright sand: geometries of iridescence,
    facets of light: sunbathers spot the beach like measles.

We march rescue reels in rectangles round the beach;
    play out line overhead, endure taunts: dickheads, wankers.

Harry throws his clothes from an upstairs window, tip-toes
    down the stairs: 'I'll ring her when I get to Perth.'

Naked, Big Bill 'Tiny' Douglass, skin like rhino hide, pads his workshop,
    turns wood, swings his balls like leather bells.

Shouting 'a meat tray and two chooks, twenty cents a ticket',
    squeezing through slabs of men thigh to thigh in the public bar.

Fleeing criss-cross down Curlewis Street, the outwitted,
    outraged chef from the Dragon's Gate puffing close behind.

Clouds ghost by, shadows articulate like sharks,
    bluebottles mass and drift with fierce intent.

Unwinged, he drops from a steepling wave
    and foresees the outcome. The sea is light in layers,
        stars maze and flicker within the foam.

※

In the hollow of a wave
    these particulars, what they can sustain.

Draped in rain, rescue reels and their unwound canvas belts
    make ready aye ready on the cast-off beach.

Waves loom, pitch, and fall like sheets of rubble,
    the sea floor shudders, faultlines tremble up the beach.

Basso combs the sand, stirs a patch of weed
    with his toe. You usually turn up something after storms.

Tunnels stretch beneath the promenade like probing fingers,
   rot, slime, rats, shadow, green and guilty smells.

Ramsgate Avenue, Brighton Boulevarde, grow second storeys,
   sprout sundecks, plate glass, cumquats, gas barbecues.

The pavilion gets another coat of paint, another yellow,
   fades, looks just about the same.

The sun pulsates, swells, draws in upon the earth, the sea,
   dreaming neither before or after, ripples, stirs.
   A man lies on his stomach in the sand,

positions his arms like fins beneath his head,
   passes into iconography. Light sifts reflective lures
      to reel me in, they reel me in.

Monster

I can't get my head around it. How did we devise

a concept like just war: *the slain of the Lord*
are dung upon the ground. I know there are distinctions
it is important to make and I don't expect perfection
but the chicanery of subtle thought ... if I pick it all apart
will anything be left to sew back into sense?

Cleverer minds are reconciled. Cultured, poised,
the government official (Should I give him spectacles?
Should they reflect the light?) pauses and replies:
The President regrets ... but consider the alternative ...

would you offer succour ... And I can almost understand.

I sleep with reason as my lover, wake beside a monster
in my bed. I fumble beneath the mask, shape my lips
to the prospect of a kill, feel your thigh
against my rump, your fingers at my throat.

Oh, Rakosi, I'm still strumming on my lyre. Is there really
so much wrong with that? I'm embarrassed

by the flimsiness of my resolve, the silliness of saints and monsters,
conversations with a being who can't plausibly exist,
this mockery of flagellation: this is my defective heart,
this my amputated foot, this the bandage from around my head.

A monster dies in the middle of his trial, another
denies the power of the court, two more evade arrest:
in politic's parlour game, each day annuls the last.

9/11, I say, and Afghanistan, Bali and Iraq,
but I can't fix a year to each event, what is,
what well might be, are steam against a bathroom mirror.
I see bits, an eye but not its double, the other ear,

a chin that lacks a jawbone for support.

Narcissus : self-portrait with sea

Waves glide in this morning full and shapely,
fashioned to grace the bay's own curves,
rising and subsiding as though breathing:
the sea as lover waking drowsily from sleep,
reaching for the sand, dreamily slipping back.

Yesterday the sea was grief and shattered glass.
It pitched against itself, railed at cliffs,
clawed retreating sand: the sea as daemon,
gouging the pretence of dreams: a whirligig
of uncompleted gestures, unpredicted ends.

This is the link. Between these days we are
the connection. Memory and the memory
of time. Hope. Beauty and the disappointments.
We are in but never of the sea, never — a silly phrase —
at one. When he gasped to see himself reflected,
that ancestor little knew the quandary he embraced.

Our eyes negotiate a shimmering, mimic surface,
make out rips, tides, and it's easy to imagine
seeing as unveiling, commensurate. What investment
have I made in this? With what do I invest it?
Estimations of force and speed, such understandings,
and with something of myself. But the sea is more than
akin to, different from. Am I even implicated?
We're apt to lose ourselves, or lose it in ourselves.

I make myself weather-wise, water-tight.

The elemental things still cling.

To be an intersection, to feel abundance
in this swell and heave, the observer of yourself
as self and as a figure clutching here, falling
and hanging on, fearful and in love.

I see all this. It happens around and to me,
seconds welling in the lungs, weight and weightlessness,
a relentless pressure down. You can't sink deep enough
to salvage calm, here no flowers bloom, stones don't speak,
neither Echo nor my twin stares back at me. Sand explodes,
water pummels and I am like a clump of weed.
Here we are material and evanescent, body
against and through the bodily. And on the surface

nothing's reflected in the foam. It would drag me down again.

Half-glimpsed through water

What was that?

From the corner of my eye,
through light's slant dismemberment,
the unsettled heft of swell, something
appears and now disappears. I dare not,
and do each time I turn my head.
It could be was or will be. I look again.

Sea's plunge, contingent maze of grey,
a pale sun too impressed to
plumb the soundings. Here, up close,

things blur as if there is an end in mind.

Anything which lacks a body
does not exist, everything which exists
has a body of its own. Is it here, this,
a figuring which is all of me?

Now's a place to put this, it's not
beyond understanding; but what to know
of how time acts between each detail, of if.
Was that a fin? Were there two?

I listen to my body.
I'm flayed, erotic, fifty metres,
thirty seconds from the cliff.

I feel you at my skin like kelp.

This disenchanted world

*... you raised me up so that I could see that there was
something to be seen, but also that I was not yet able to see it.*
                              St Augustine

If the lake is an eye, misshapen,
blue-bleeding, fed by a tracery of streams,
then sea is an allegory of sight, shallow transparency
or vast opacity swallowing pterygiums of land. Lake and sea
see nothing, are seen by, from vantage points.

Seagulls fly to the beach to bask in summer,
and the colony of pelicans to stand still as totems
on the basalt island, the wind that swept through the night
carrying nothing visible, the faint pulse of waves
that swell and flop on the jiggling feet of children.
Beyond the headland an illusory line demarks green from blue
and whitecaps plunge and disappear like ice bobbing in a thaw.

The strict discipline of all this formlessness,
the lines of swell, the lines of children,
the north-east wind tracking down the coast,
the pelicans and seagulls on the sand,
birds following the leader in that mesmerising 'v';
that plane – balanced between propulsion and gravity's
weak force – measured against my own inertia.

This coming back or coming to the coast, to caravans,
sandflies, mosquitoes, sunburn and cantankerousness.
Yet nothing is irksome in the sweat of the night,
the popping of tin, the scratch of banksia, dreams,
the instress and stuttering before we grasp at air.

Time waits behind the dunes, the scrubby hills as,
in summer's sweet postponement, we stalk our better selves.

We have evolved this far, to come to the edge
of the sea, to play like dolphins emerging
and submerging, hanging on like tangled mangrove roots,
black eroded cliffs, sun-dried coastal daisies, awake to
the high machinery of cicadas through the heat,
the electric charge that skips along a wavelet's rim
when a ripple going out ignites a ripple coming in,
the angles of deflection as this common light
lips waves, lards itself on sand, plays shadows with the leaves
(the last falling and rising): it blinds my watching eye,
my making sense, my expecting to see.

In the lake a mother swings her daughter round and round,
her trailing hair; her trailing legs: summer: radiating to every shore.

Monster

I thought I'd done with you, given up

the nostalgia of disgust. Of what earthly use
is this dossier of fact and speculation,
the tut tut tut or, for some, the leap
that precludes an end — *only acknowledge
thine iniquity, that thou hast transgressed.*

'Evolvere' is to unroll
and it's not like that — we mutate
and never change at all. We are words

balanced on a plinth of words: that sparrow is the devil,
that one carries truth, the raven is up to covert tricks
in the best of alternative worlds. (Have you heard the one

about the cosmologists drinking beer?
'The more it's comprehensible,' Weinberg says,
'the more it's cold and pointless.'

'And the more I see a law-like order,'
Paul Davies mutters from his glass.) I am not

a soul in the darkness of the world but,
let's face it, this isn't working, there is no
bloodless blood, no wafer unalloyed.

Against the livid orange sunset, consolation
(Is it a wing? A fuselage?) dips behind the hill,
out of the debris: fragments, disconnected things,
suffering that makes nothing holy.

Spring is still spring (summer)

The mid-summer sea is flat; and now mid-winter cold.

Nor'easterlies have drawn the southern current
up and in. We talk about it, can't remember
such a betrayal of bargains we consider struck.

The day itself is wet with heat, squeezed
as if everything, us, houses on the cliffs, clouds,
could melt and intermix, become hot ooze.

Have you had a happy life? 'Well, yes,' the poet murmurs
'I have, I mean ...' Mind re-orders time,

fixes and leaves behind the silliness of hope.
The common toad may not come back; eight thousand skulls
are a pyramid near Phnom Penh. I look away

And when I look back it's like those pictures
of divine breath emanating from a cloud,
whitecaps flicker, the sea ripped open and as suddenly
restored. From this shore there's distraction for the eye
but no immediate promise. Tomorrow

the world won't be a safer or a fairer place,
our willingness to wonder and to hurt will be the same.
But the sea may come up and, if we're lucky
and not too afraid, we might press ourselves
against the edge of that one big wave, cling and let go.

Collusion (2012)

'Is it better to be here or there?'

Daniel Defoe, *Robinson Crusoe,*
(Chapter 4 'First Weeks on the Island')

***

Dear K, it's light that makes the river flow, or seem to flow.
Efflorescence skipping from crest to crest as though it were a school of tiny fish

and disappearing beneath a bridge. A bolted, welded, seconds-long eclipse and then it flickers back again.

It's harder to count than stars. More subject to vagaries, fancy, the weakness of belief. Is it matter

or does it depend on matter's movement, the hardly more substantial lifting it and losing it in troughs? Most of the time

I think like this, unsure what can exist without an imprint. My reflection stutters in the windows of a speeding train and then I'm looking at a field of sheep,

black-faced and lazily intent. The glimmerings are flecks of time. I can't decide whether they are truly in the moment or moments out of time, essence or deviation from the path.

There's no conclusion here, no resolution myth. Things rise up and fall away as if they never were, rise up again. I like the dancing light,

the scattered cloud, the river that lies potentially between its banks, the speeding train. I reach for them. They reach for me.

*
**

After the lassitudes of blue, the sun: now buttermilk,
now brimful and overflowing, suddenly fierce and red,

about to slip below the chipped and crenellated grime,
but shimmering for this last instant before becoming

those shades of pink that bless and surely must amaze,
dusk an uncertain premise, premonition which cannot last

much longer. The world is swaddled now in undertones,
the rhymes we chant to put an end to doubt,

to all that is mysterious and temptingly unknowable.
To think about a mystery we must imagine it.

maybe as a labyrinth or maze, as forest or lantana stand
but not as nothing or the thing impenetrable,

                              that would have another tangled name.

Something passes by, you turn but nothing's there except,
perhaps, a disturbance in the air, a wobble in the orbit

of a distant world, the glint in an oceanic vent.
Free diving is not entirely free: to go down you leave behind:

and coming back breath is an unremitting currency:
constrained air hammers for release, bubbles rise, burst,

or momentarily make transparent domes
which float the sting beneath. Nothing is defined

in all this visibility. Here matter is miraculous again,
wind a devil's breath, silence a wing in the shuffling air.

Such commingling could be eternity, a beyond beyond all seeing
unravelling heart's battle with time that curves and disappears

in pettifogging words. When day grows dark and unintended
is it better to sense or see? The externality of things, that is enough,

it admits of hidden roots, sap which rises,
bark that strips and burns, the complicated exchange of air,

       even the whole tree that falls unnoticed.

Impossible to think 'black' or 'blank'. To think of any thing
that is not thing: black maw, black hood,

blank slate waiting to be filled. Light is sifted through the clouds,
highlights then deflects. Close your eyes. The invisible

saying now, now, 'you', an insect on a lake, a moth on glass,
the stealth of ocean currents, waves that feather in the wind,

the merest touch. You open your mouth to cry and a bird flies out.
Another and another. They arrange themselves in rank and order,

drop like stones. The sea responds with holes. If this is it,
if there is nothing more, then nothing must be more,

what is not cannot be. Hold my hand. We are strange uncertain beasts,
rooted to this place, singing without conviction

until a landscape intervenes. We shrink against the hills,
are lost in the verticals of trees, the clutch and merge of waves,

                                           our voices drowning in this curious light.

It's almost spring in our neglected hemisphere.
As yet no indication we've tilted far enough
to receive the annual, waited-for reward.
The sea and sky volley what there is of dusk
and a peevish wind plays nip and tuck
to irritate the waves. In its own good time
the sun will be here and the sea all aquamarine
as if, overnight, spirit could manifest as light
and just this startling colour. Then morning warmth,
leaves on imported trees, poems (God help us!),
and mothballs for our heavy winter clothes.
And we are lighter too. Do we deserve it?
No. But the punishing and forgiving world
will give it to us anyway and I'll give thanks
though to whom or what it's useless to inquire.

In the hour or so before night's certain fall,
as light cuts loose the day and heat relents,
the body recalls what it is to breathe and sometimes
the mind finds pleasure in teeming emptiness.
Today there are no shadows and particulars
are soft with lack of definition. The jacaranda
against the church's mortared, crumbling mass,
mauve and stunning and substantial as it is —
all indirect flowering of twists and turns —
seems uncontained, as though at any moment
it might escape the rooted, understandable restraints
of space and time and float away as weightless
as a dandelion on the emerging evening breeze.

***

Waking at night silence has the colour
that is all colours, or none at all. Gradually
the dark gives presence to
intangibles that sway and waver

in the narrow space between curtains
and the window, between wall and open door,
among the clothes tossed so carelessly
on the straight-backed chair as if, last night,

nothing mattered except the need to sleep,
to inhabit silence. Now silence is an alien state
and I am on its rim, sensing rather than seeing
something for which I can't conceive a name.

There's nothing here. This is not a ghost story,
not a horror flick, not even a remnant
of the culture, history that makes one reach
for notions like 'apprehension of the divine'.

I am here and bodily so, just still
and more than usually aware, an awareness
that depends upon the nearby edge of sleep,
circumstance rather than an act of will.

What do I hope to touch in this
secluded secret place where I now intrude,
shifting everything so noticeably, imperceptibly,
even in my attentive immobility, my desire

not to interfere. I am the observer,
scientist of states and matter.
If I wished I could break this silence,
crack it against my skull, but instead

I hold it poised
in an unvoiced, lingering embrace
as if near-perfection could exist within
or out there somewhere unforeseen.

In the sound-excluded room
there remains the heart, its muted beat,
and off-timed breath, now shallow,
now submarine and slow. My mind is silent too

and still. I can't describe it. Not empty
like some vessel, not grey and wispy
like a fog: something more substantial,
not set and settled but curiously serene,

like breathing starlight. What might this be?
And if I held my breath? Would this be like
putting a hand against your heart to count
its intervals, delay what mostly is inevitable?

Light jostles through the trees
and wrestles to be heard. It's insistent
but hardly comprehensible, a re-connection
that dislocates as surely as it joins.

※

All morning it's been difficult to settle, difficult to harness
        energy or purpose for all the things
                I have to do. Charged sky,

sudden light at the horizon, grey, then streaks of blue, then
        grey again. An unsettled sea,
                white water contending point to point,

waves like another and another avalanche, unceasing noise,
        sand compacted to a crimp-edged,
                man-high bank and I can see,

then can't locate, a buoy like a white-capped head
        sinking and floating in the rip,
                wrenched from its deeper mooring,

now driven in, now swept back out, tethered there
        by net and anchor that, for now,
                have new purchase in the sand.

Conceivably, should I be silly enough to surf tomorrow
        it could be me entangled, drowned:
                mistake and misadventure, bad luck.

In Switzerland they've flicked the switch and particles
        surge round and round a tunnel
                in opposed directions preparing to collide

in an experiment to explain how the universe got mass
        in the seconds of its birth,
                why what we touch is solid.

We stalk the irreducible, the constant speed of light unfolding
           though the eye can't see and the hand
                      can't touch such magnitude:

time may shrivel, outrun itself, sag under accumulated weight:
                end in our beginning: red shift, white dwarf,
                      rotten apple on the ground.

A low pressure cell is tracking up the coast.
Already the sky and road are an equal grey
and the sea is only visible because the bay
is choked with the white of broken waves.
TV cables swing like skipping ropes and street signs
shiver in the pillaging wind. Not a bird in the sky
but strangely the clouds are still, too heavy
or too high to move. It's still inside the house;
but for the wind against the windows it's quiet as well.
The baby is asleep. Every now and then his eyelids twitch
and his lips make pucking sounds, or he draws in
a deeper than expected breath. Six weeks old
and swaddled in his cot mid-afternoon. Dreaming,
I suppose. He'll wake and play, and maybe smile
though what the smile might mean, if anything,
is a further adult supposition. For now he's warm and settled,
not inert, but sheltered from the wildness all around.

*
**

I remember very little, a lingering fear that I was drowning —
    my mouth was open and I was mumbling. 'No, please' —
    but what it might mean

I have no idea, if, indeed, meaning has meaning except in the
    most restricted sense, the means by which we manage the
    dailiness of lives. It's philosophy isn't it,

the thinking that can think about any thing, the realisation
    thought can be experienced but the mind can not,

and if, think of it, mind's imaginary like Albino Island, Adam's
    Country, Atlantis, Moore's Utopia,

even Hat Pins in Rootabaga Country where all the hat pins in
    the world are made,

then we can manufacture anything, spin it out of nothing,
    scraps and memories lived and overheard, the mind as
    virtual as the web.

I wonder what he meant, the one who said, 'True places never
    are on any map.' That can't be true. It scares, yet still
    appeals. Where was the white whale formed?

Once, T-O maps split the world between Noah's sons, encircled it
    with sea, and forbade a southern continent to abide.

Once, from his cell, Fra Mauro inked stories on his maps and as
    he drew repeatedly declared, 'it now exists.'

Why should this remind me of one manifestation of the church, a
   pastor saying, 'The visible is transitory, the invisible endures'

in reference not to Logos but to shady, worldly deals? What was
   coursing through that mind

or mine? I don't know where I'm going here, lack even an
   embellished map, my thinking like that of sailors sighting
   stars from ships adrift on wrongly charted seas.

I keep thinking of Lowell's simple line – 'My mind's not right.' So
   stark, yet still uncertain beside the unthinking thinking of
   his skunk,

or Ted Hughes' hawk, rehearsing perfect kills. Was I ever skunk
   or hawk, or always second-guessing prey to doubt.

the figure at the looking-glass of consciousness where eyes stare
   back and I stare back ... I suppose we're all the same,

every now and then suspect the world might be communal
   story, syntax the ship we sail from Serendib to Sydney,

scratchings that fade and disappear on successive pages of the
   map and, dangerously, I start to think time, the outside
   world might be inside my head.

Was I even thinking when I dreamt last night? Awake, conscious,
   I know it wasn't real, thinking now and thinking back,

and looking at that white cloud which seems to swell and could
   be, but isn't, a monstrous breaking wave – it's my best
   surmise of what there is.

*
**

I want to say the word 'adrift'. It seems important. But even as
    my tongue clicks up against the final 't'

my mind's submerged in cinematic kitsch, a wide shot of the
    empty sea, the speck that is a raft, the lips that are always
    caked and cracked.

Below me, real time now, the coastline flexes in interrupted lengths
    and, among the stranded rocks and broken slabs of cliff,

the sea's fetch is checked, it's looming force subdivided into suck
    and swirl and white scribbles on blue sheets

and I'm wondering where it comes from and where IT goes and
    why I've written IT.

'Write all of everything that is known', a Chinese Emperor
    instructed his encyclopaedists but I know so little,

hold to even less, worry that conviction might be convincing but
    beside the point and so have no response except,

'it may be so.' Mallarmé suggested, 'One must set things straight.
    There must always be enigma.' This also may be so.

I try to make sense of IT, wonder how we postulate a time
    when time began but have only disputed endings as a
    consequence. If I'm not careful I'll be quoting Heraclitus

who really begs a thousand questions and can't account for Pi or
    Fibonacci numbers or why, if I were to say,

we cling to the past like sailors to a sinking raft, you might reply,
    the future is a hologram

flung from a window on the fortieth floor. In the flicker-flacker
    of the light, the leaf-whip banter of the trees, the physics of
    teeming streets and high glass walls,

faces announce and supersede themselves, each fixed and
    fleeting, true and just as likely false.

Here are feet walking down the street, a shadow stretched
    behind and a glass-gripped man – abreast, apace – looking
    left as you look right.

Perhaps he'll notice the stem and webbing of this boat-shaped
    leaf flinching in the wind, sun sneaking through the foliage,
    the skitter and flash

of small imagined life scurrying through the undergrowth, the
    unthinkability of 'no thing' even in the unheard, unseen,
    we-can't-be-sure, misleadings of the light.

When Basho wrote 'Nothing in the cicada's cry suggests they
    are about to die' he cast a thought whose concentric
    circles may never reach the shore of time.

✳︎
✳︎✳︎

You know the way a snatch of song lodges in your brain and won't
 be shifted no matter how you try to trick it out the door?

Well, this morning 'Amazing Grace' has come to stay, just the
 tune and those two words; the bits about 'no sweeter sound'
 and 'save a wretch like me'

disregarded somewhere else. Which is not so strange as I don't
 believe in 'lost' and 'saved' but I do know forms of grace exist

and are amazing. I think of a dancer's grace as she glides into the
 air, or the diver's equal grace gliding towards the sea: the
 body in defiance of its limitations,

going through, beyond. Graceful, gracious, gracile, words that
 multiply and spread like a flowering vine. Grace notes of
 unbelief that still restore the faith.

I'd like to be standing by the laundry door looking at snow piled
 high in the backyard and stretching away to distant hills, all
 deep silence and soft light,

indistinctions that are pliable and hint at more and more
 concealment. Here, today, each leaf and branch is clear, and
 even shadows are

unsentimentally direct. Surface is baked surface and heat haze
 won't bear comparison with mist, won't let me think
 transcendence.

The following is true. The water in the bay is pristine, amazing
shades of green, a random morse of light, the sea flushing
between rocks with a gentle pop and splash

that avoids monotony. But in the channel, among the leaves and
weed and scraps of paper, two dead seabirds – black and
bloated – bob in the push and pull,

their wings flared and fixed in mimicry of flight, their feet flexed
as though they were about to land.

And now I'm stuck in the feedback loop: adrift in sun, snow,
amazing grace, dead birds. The binary brain looking for a
way out or in between,

a way to celebrate without appearing selfish or simple-minded,
without me at the centre pulling strings or getting out the
bubble wrap,

without an image of the imageless, or an image of the world
devoid of people to make the whole thing work, the dream,

uncalled for, undeserved, of the present expanding as if there
is no future or the future is this presence, that leafless
tree against the sky,

the glittering humpbacked sea, the thousand flickering things
the mind lights on and tries to hold.

I can eclipse you with a wink, Donne wrote
and yes, when we close our eyes matter melts
into the absence behind our lids as if, blindly,
we were staring at, or were, eclipse, a dark centre
and the dance of flames around the rims, imagined heat,
imagined light, one step closer to becoming not hollow
but invisible, figures whose existence must be inferred
by sound, by the accoutrements we drape around
our formless forms, or by consequent disturbance
as we pass, an effacement so complete we cease to be
or exist as emanation, that sense we provoke in others
of otherworldliness, a thing which can't be thing
but still is thought to be, that sees but is not seen.

***

Contested ground, this strange persistent beauty
which sticks even as it passes, the crocodile scales
of the bloodwood's trunk, the snow gum's pale
and sensuous length, the sun working its light
through shadow to the grasstree's tip, or dancing
like rain or phosphorescence on a barely moving sea.
Is it now misleading to think sustaining, true?

I look through leafless, sunset-blackened trees
to a pink and orange sky laid out like a proposition
composed of all the fleeting possibilities before the eye:
the lick of cloud that might almost be a sign,
birds which tack and weave before lighting on a course,
the lingering slips of blue just now passing into memory.
What is seen is merely seen, if anything so beautiful
can manifest without desire, without this leaping up
like a fish, like a heart, like a flickering thought
which can't be hooked, or tricked, into another light.

Past and future tussle and the shrinking present
intervenes to push them back apart. Time seems
a one-way flight, seems to come again, and beauty
keeps its counsel, out-thinks our simple-minded words.
Here forgetfulness and memory play ludo with desire.

A white cockatoo above a railway line,
a daylight moon masquerading as a ghost.
Inside the gut a microbe multiplies, burrows deeper,
hooks on to an unsuspecting host and waits.
Crabs with eight thousand eyes clatter across mudflats
and we dream robots looking back from miles in space.

What clandestine patterns time and thought
fall into without time or thought at all,
the legerdemain by which I fancy I am a sufficient,
co-incidental thing, skin, my border, coming into contact
with other skin which touches and retreats,
touches and retreats, flinches at the little slights,
the acts of spite and meanness, the ancient sin of pride,
guilt which eats away. Imagine, my love,
an outbreak of silence, and how the respite of 'now'
would be hounded by 'once', 'soon', 'again'.

Dear K, I tire of the apparatus of my brain.
I fear that you (my interlocutor, my will,
my conscience) may also tire. The thoughts I think
have passed their use-by dates, are petals tossed
in Burnt Norton's dusty wind. We could,
we probably do, lead many lives even as
an inoffensive clerk or as a monstrous insect
squirming on its back, feet and feelers wildly
seeking purchase on the air. We stand accused.
We answer allegations we make against ourselves.

❦

Someone finding this will think I'm corresponding
with Franz Kafka (it could be Kierkegaard
or Krazy Kat), I'm not that mad, and besides,
Kafka had too many problems of his own (migraines, boils,
constipation, tuberculosis, a certain paranoia).
Perhaps I should write a self-help book or start a cult,
any alien explanation will hook a few unwary souls.

❦

I fear infirmity, loss of speech, dependence,
know I lack the stoic touch, the grip
which makes some hold and hold unwavering.
I will go gently. Not because life is painful now
or was or holds no pleasures more but for the beauty
I have had. Wattle-birds calling from a banksia tree,
the complexity of fern and flannel flower, a lizard
whose mottled back is moss against a fallen limb,
those touches; a sea breeze which helps the skin remember.

❦

Now, suddenly, I'm awake to rain
cascading through the trees and successive waves
of thunder strike with all the force of dream.
The heart leaps up again and does not lack
though it knows so much must slip away
and there is no certainty from which to plead.

It appears we are machines to manufacture words,
each weighted with deliberation or floating crosswise
on currents of uncertainty. Seabirds swoop,
plunge through an interlocking edge, come away
with wriggling fish between their beaks or nothing,
either way a penetration of that collusion,
surface-glued-to-surface, which signals difference,
one side, the lean, light-strutted transparency of flight,
the other a grayscale, ever-deepening dark: at best
a hard-won buoyancy. Lie back, you say, trust
the density of matter, the way the sun can warm
even as the sea enfolds you in a cool embrace:
displacement, though it almost feels like home.
Words leave. Air and water rush to fill the space.

※

In the background there is the music that almost always
accompanies someone running down the street,
or a narrow, dusk-darkened alleyway between
the fire escapes of tenements, alone or gripping,
one step behind, his girlfriend's hand. Their faces,
stricken, swivel ever more frantically as time
looks down on what neither you nor they can see.

Soon they may not be. The angels are out on strike,
that's a black car swinging into sight and filling
the street kerb to kerb. The headlights flare and stupidly
we freeze. How did we get here? What must happen next?
Let it be. An hour ago none of this existed. An hour ago
if you looked through one of those windows just now
catching the day's last light you would have seen us

tangled in each other and the storm-rucked sheets
of a cast iron bed. A ceiling fan would be a touch too many.
We're sated and asleep. This can't be innocence and you know
there will be a price to pay. Time passes by and outside
pigeons are scratching in the gutters, dogs are sniffing at garbage cans
and, somewhere else, a hard-faced man picks up the telephone,
listens, nods, says one word and, laying the receiver gently

back in its cradle, stares though the fourth wall
into the muddled middle distance of his imagination
seeing, we can't know, an ideal past, an awful present,
what will surely be. We turn and run to where we've been
but dark-suited men step round a corner and advance towards us.
We stop again. Look for a passageway to the left, the damaged door
we can shoulder open. This time it won't budge. This time…

*
**

Gloom off to the west. And blowing in my direction like
        mounting slow-motion waves are banks of deep grey cloud.

I ride towards them. Pedal-stroke by pedal-stroke the odds of
        getting wet, and soon, are getting worse.

The air now curt and chill, and in a flurry the first raindrops
        are flicked against my arms, then swept away.

The body moves forward. The body holds still. Mind rattles
        back and forth and catches on itself. The legs drive on.

Think ahead, I caution. Look left and right, both near and far.
        But I'm stuck on the mechanics of wheels: the axle, the
        thin tube of swollen air

in contact with the ground, friction's retardation, the end-in-
        its-beginning rim skimming relativities between the fact of things.

We can't go back, though we're apt to waver even as our
        wheels spin on. Behind me the memory of a Malvern
        Star, that hill, failing brakes, a broken chain, and flying

backside-down-feet-first through a neighbour's hedge, broken
        bones and proof of the interplay of mass and force, the
        physics of stop and go,

that a body in motion tends to stay in motion unless ... There's
        still uncertainty in what is certain, postulates of indecision,
        laughter, or an unexpected cry.

Time flits off or closes in and the space between me and a
    drenching shrinks. Wheels slip and wobble and up ahead

it's possible to see rain stiffen into spears and, more fancifully,
    coalesce into a solid-seeming wall.

I race towards it expecting in some unlikely way to escape the
    unrelenting clutch of earth. I'm mad, you say?

How so? Light splits the clouds in silver streaks, trees leap to cheer
    me on, clap their soft green hands in wild excitement,

and the future is an endlessness of blue. On the road behind me, a
    ghost bike takes up the chase. It's closing fast.

I walk among the dead. Trimmed and untrimmed graves,
symbols I think are Gaelic, and hosts of Guardian Angels,
some with heads lopped off, chipped smocks, shattered wings.
The morning sun flings light across the sea and, to the eye,
each cross is turned to black. Here lie the much beloved
unknown wives, adored fathers, children gone too soon,
vaults and edifices where family feuds subside.
Six mostly intact angels stand beside one pathway.
All their heads are bowed but this one presses flowers
to her belly, this one scatters blossoms from the basket
of her gown, this one's arms are folded on her breasts,
and this one's palms are lightly pressed in prayer.
This one shelters one child, this one two. And on this last,
brown head twitching, a sparrow has momentarily perched.

Autumn warmth is draining from the day
though we'll be right in T-shirts for a while.
Two dogs nip each other, take turns
to turn their bellies up in a gentle patch of light,
and the rolling hiss of rubber, the clack of trams
take on, you won't believe me, the tone of lullaby.
All day I've drifted in this contented sea,
seen nothing I didn't like, heard not a single
angry word – conditions of the atmosphere
at a certain time and place. Were I a fisherman
fish would surely be swimming up my line.
Soon it will be night. We'll twist about an axis in our beds
(and wake as though the sun had circled thus for us).

*
**

I almost understand this resonance, this hum
or echo which I can only picture as a frequency,

oscillations expanding and diminishing
from a single source. And the sometime static

which crackles and interrupts, which implies
another source, another thought or possibility.

It comes when dragonflies shimmer in an afternoon's
blue heat or when you're watching drifting birds

and say to yourself, silently aloud, their wings
absorb the sunlight, make deals with the wind.

It's like that curious deep-breath sensation when,
diving on a weed-enfolded reef, you surrender

to the slew and sweep of swell and your body,
that bounded unreliable, actual fact,

loosens the skin's tight grip so you are
and, simultaneously, you are not.

It's not persistent but too here and now
to be dismissed as fleeting. We are called back to

our other selves, to the commonplace again.
My grandchild stirs in the back seat of the car,

rubs his eyes then settles down to sleep again,
his chest rising and falling as the air

slips in and out, in and out, through the
open mouth and snaggle teeth. This day

is wet and hot and beads of sweat
have collected on his forehead. His tangled hair

is as orange as a mimic sun and his fingers
rest upon his knees like dreaming lizards.

And here's Mark Strand, my while-I'm-waiting book:
so many poems about expecting to die,

and night and dark and, yes, a little light.
When my grandson wakes we'll race into the pool,

he'll splash and squeal and burble and fling himself
off the edge, kick his legs and almost swim.

⁂

Rain as it is only brighter. Momentarily the luminous is
    threading through the grey. So tempting to affirm:

the commonplace is beautiful and still surprising. Now
    glistening shades of green, the pure white

crumpled flowers, there the purple I thought black, and deeper
    all the hidden, tangled world: might unbearable be that
    which must be borne,

what can't be shed or shucked? Nearby a voice says, with all my
    heart; someone else can't speak at all; and the rain keeps
    coming down.

Almost everything can be explained. We forget, choose not to
    think, or in the moment

surrender to an incessant we know will pass, mystery with as
    many forms as birds have different wings.

Dear K, this particular rain is here at last and we are wet and
    alive and laughing

that in all this pitiless world what touches us now with its
    unbidden grace, its dripping material thingitude, is just
    this rain.

Have Been and Are (2016)

... a secret transaction, a voice answering a voice
Virginia Woolf, *Orlando*

And the word 'environment'
such a bloodless word, a flat-footed word
Joy Williams

It's not about me ... and of course
it is. There's a dappled light falling
across my forearms as it has fallen

many times before and will, I imagine, fall again.
Mmm ... there's that word 'dappled', that won't do.
It's not a bad word, it does the job,

you know what it means and what
my arms look like, patched with light and shade,
but still it won't do. This book is all about

how lucky I am to be walking under these trees,
through this scrub just metres from the cliff
and the blue unknowns of the sea, lucky and I hope

not ungrateful no matter how you might construe
that gratitude. Ted Kooser composed
one hundred poems called Winter Morning Walks

as he recovered from cancer and sent them
to that other poet of the prairie and the plain, of the
inner and the outer life, Jim Harrison.

You're my reader. I appeal to you, I owe you
this explanation. It's summer. It's early morning,
the light is gentle through the trees though later

it will be punishing. I am the odd one out,
the visitor, the one who looks and leaves
and makes some human sense, some human use,

of what has no use for me, my forearms
in the dappled light. A mare is dappled
or a cow. Little children ride a mare

or milk a piebald cow. What alternatives might there be:
sprinkled? blotted? mottled? variegated?
'Variegated'! So much worse, not a speck

of colour, not a fleck of blood or mulch or sense.
The sea's in front of me, the endless, pulsing,
not to be assumed, reassuring sea,

and behind, through the trees and not to be denied,
a bitumen block of streets and rows of re-defined,
reconstructed cottages of this south coast town.

It's quiet. It's still. The only sounds are birdcall,
cicada trill, the mysteries of what is scurrying,
my footfall on brittle, broken twigs. My horizon

is barred by trees, not barred but complicated,
the rough, misshapen, stunted trunks and
every-which-way branches splitting up sky and sea.

I pass saw-leafed banksias and scarlet
grevillea blooms, pass a bush with yellow berries
and one with black, one with fronds that sweep and sway

like insect feelers, another whose tips are curled
and curlicued like supple springs, sudden buds of white
and cream, red leaves among the green and brown;

pass over all that is fallen, criss-cross, haphazard, all
that we have categorized which is just bush to me.
And here's another bird I don't know, tiny, grey,

red-crested with another flash of red beneath his tail,
hopping foot to foot almost at my feet. A finch?
Is it mad to be writing 'bird' and 'leaf', 'tree' and 'sea'

in this post-post-post Romantic age? American poets
write about snow, chipmunks or deer, mountains. Sometimes
they write about the writing which writes itself.

They are all professors. They teach half the year
and spend the other half at a cabin in the woods
or their apartment in Rome. It seems, blissfully,

a divided life. Except Harrison and Kooser
and a hundred or so others I might name,
exceptions which will do to make this rule.

Glory be to God for dappled things —
                              For skies of couple-colour as a brinded cow.
It's not a competition, I know, but heavens

how do you compete with Hopkins? *Couple-colour!*
Whatever is fickled, freckled! It could make you weep
with joy for such exuberance, such celebration.

We, I, have learned to lose these sentiments, we've learned
distance, irony, we question god or man's dominion,
his right to name and claim, to cut down, dig up,

despoil. *In God's wildness*, John Muir wrote,
lies the hope of the world. And even in this little patch
of coastal scrub, this scruffy in-between of sand and stone,

of stiffening bark and insect-eaten leaves, there is hope,
sharp as salt, gritty as sand, flickering, shadowy hope.
Look up. Follow the silk-skinned, bark-shed scribbly gums

making for the sun. Look down. To the finely excavated
mounds of ants, the moss and mushrooms on fallen branches
and the lichen, ferns and grasses. Where are the words

I need to think these things which have no need
of thought, to write a landscape which is mute, which murmurs
of silence, the unimportance of each step.

༂

It seems the origin of 'dapple' (dappled)
is uncertain, it might be Icelandic: 'depill'
for 'spot' or 'dot'; a name for a dog, an affectionate

abbreviation for Dorothy. I seem to be off the track
but now I'm winding down, clinging to trunks
and branches and stretching rock to rock

as the bush dips towards the sand and skips
a stream that is swirling out against the tide,
against little waves which lift and stall

before crumpling on the beach with a rumble
which always makes them sound much bigger.
The sea is full of these deceptions, sudden gutters,

hidden rocks, rips which wax and wane, drifts
and currents to drag you from your course. How then
can I call it 'reassuring?' *The swimmer can say,*

Bachelard wrote, *the world is my will; the world is
my provocation. It is I who stir up the sea.* What nonsense!
He can't have swum against a rip for what seems

like hours and not moved what seems an inch,
or been held down by wave after wave as the strength
drains from his arms and his lungs burn

for lack of air … Where am I?
Oh, still standing on the beach just looking
at the sea and this should be all about a walk

just for pleasure and the dappled light, not
to make some point about how we write ourselves
into environment, wilderness; shape the world

into our words. It's inevitable. Best to acknowledge
when we're doing it. So, I pass through bush, I tread upon;
I am within the sea, wrapped round, held. Is it

just me? This is a morning poem, a summer poem,
it wants to take you by the hand and say
'Come, come with me into this environment,

this moment and these meanderings, notice
this half-buried rock persisting, a Yellow Robin
hunting, a Fairy Wren calling to his mate,

that goanna soaking up the sun.' But now it's time
for me to make my way back, follow my shadow
up the hill and beyond the baffle of trees, to step flat-footedly

towards the rising sound of cars. I walked here yesterday
and the day before. I won't be here tomorrow. Let's not lament,
lest my words belittle the dappled light ...

Brain doesn't improvise

brain thinks, fingers go where brain will not
Elena Kats-Chernin

There are minds which think in straight lines,
sentences, and others, like mine, which like diversions,
think in fragments, spin round and round in identical
or ever-diminishing spirals, spinning or sinking
into ... what? Somewhere else? Nowhere? Silly
speculation. There is no other 'where'. The mind
is sometimes here and sometimes just not here,
in sleep mode, dream mode, memory mode, the connections
scrambled for a moment or a little longer. It's
more 'when' than 'where'. This is thinking sideways
or lying in wait so when a thought comes at you
out of left field, so to speak, all you have to do
is pounce. Easier said than done, though I've done it,
I think I have, more than once, catching my own drift ...

We are lashed to our body
the harpoon of the mind wedged in us
Linda Gregg

Thinking may begin with sound, memory,
a sight anticipated yet unseen, mis-seen,
like the tremor of wind late at night
or the play of shadow on a cloudy day,
invisible light materializing the sky's blue scope,
the green inner-outer facing of the leaves, even
the liver-brick apartments overseeing streets.
Thought might be salt right across your shoulder blades
or its faint reminder on your lips and tongue
from other lips and tongues, the tingling
that comes back and goes away, eyes that hold you
even now. For what can we do about gristle and bone,
flesh, even the figment we call 'mind',
this postcard of sandstone Buddhas denying
what the helpless body cannot help but affirm ...

The poet is a centipede
whose ability to walk depends on not thinking about how the legs work
Charles Baudelaire

The givens of the material world, the givens
of the body, what wears away or breaks or
stands the test of time. The un-givens of the mind,
so much expected of it, still so little known,
conjecture, scans, graphs, the bits of brain lit up
in all the likely, difficult-to-remember places,
amygdale, hypothalamus, hippocampus — part dolphin,
part horse, part bird — there must be others, pulses,
storms, the analogy of electric light. It doesn't
feel like that. Mostly consciousness is
unconscious like the complicated calculation
we'd require to walk or swim or love if we had
to think about it. Aldous Huxley thought one's life
a prolonged effort not to think. That's another matter ...

Body is but a striving
to become mind
Samuel Taylor Coleridge

I've got a pain behind my left knee,
another in my hip and lower back, another
in my neck. 'Pains," I say, 'go away' but in a sense
I like them. They're my body talking to me,
being sensible, saying, 'take more care.' I just wish
they wouldn't nag so much, or is that my mind?
The mind says 'no,' the body says, 'yes,' the mind
says 'oh no,' but late, too late. The wave notches up
a degree or two of steepness and all that's possible
is down, as though someone had dug a deep black hole
at the bottom of a slippery dip. My body arches
like a ballerina's, the soles of my feet strike my head.
I'm not big enough to be an obstacle water must
go round so it goes through me like a freight train
full of pillows and I'm flung and flipped and twisted,
afraid I'll hear a snap or lose all feeling
down my arm. There's hope and expectation and
a yawning gap between. The body makes up its mind ...

At the end of the mind
the body, but at the end of the body, the mind.
Paul Valery

I think I'll get a tattoo. Sixty-four
is an auspicious age. By now my skin
must have stretched and sagged and settled
far enough and any colour should last as long as me.
It's not an idle thought. It would have to be
Hokusai, *The Great Wave Off Kanagawa* climbing
up and over my left shoulder and spilling
down my chest. I couldn't do it. Not really.
I'd feel too conspicuous, too unlike myself.
I'm struggling. Is there any contradiction
between the Emersonian self and the multitudes
Whitman could contain? I don't think so
but I may be wrong and anyway
is there any way this can possibly matter.
I am one and others, sometimes other to myself,
tendrils and antennae casting about, probing,
sensing souls and soles ...

To get the better of words
for the things one no longer has to say,
T.S. Eliot

I chase a thought along the early evening street
dashing between the bumper bars of parked cars
and skittering in and out of traffic. It slips
down an alleyway with me in close pursuit,
past garbage cans, a vagrant propped against a pole,
and a bicycle which scoots in the reverse direction.
Thought pauses at a corner, looks both ways then,
just as I'm about to leap, lurches to the left.
I curse, grit my teeth and, like an overweight policeman
in a British TV drama who is outmanoeuvred
by an adolescent in a hoodie, I stumble after it.
Thought leaps two by two up the railway station steps,
vaults the ticket barrier, plunges down the escalator
and squeezes into a carriage as the automatic doors
ooze shut. Thought winks, leans back against a seat,
and I stand puffing on the platform as the 5.32 pulls out ...

The rain falls down
on last year's man. That's a Jew's harp on the table, that's a crayon in his hand.
Leonard Cohen

The reality of time ... mmm. Block universe
or ever-present present. Am I out there somewhere
perpetually re-living old insults and failed ripostes
or stupidly clutching at a 'now' perpetually
slipping from my grasp, no place from where to plot
the unconvincing fiction of myself. Light rain sprinkles
unexpectedly from a clear-blue, leaf-fringed sky, river gums
repeat in ripples, re-present as snags and sunken logs,
vines and twigs anchor deeper in the sand below.
Water striders skitter-scatter from my paddle's blade
and spiders jump aboard as the kayak nose-pokes
through reeds and over rocks rolled smooth in the shallow,
barely-flowing river. Cicada song rises and falls
in clouds of sound and rosellas flit red and green
through drab leaves. One thing after another
and simultaneously, not adding on but accruing,
being something not so hard to grasp. Inconsequences that,
for the moment, are made more. Different from
and the same as art which lives inside and outside time,
is relative, is an entitlement of fixity and flux ...

The most important experience of being
is the joy of existing
Romain Gary

Is there more or less than this? I lift my head
from reading an essay on Brother Antoninus
(he of the monkish robes and buckskin jacket)
to hear birds I can't identify singing in the eucalypts
and see about the garden a host of common butterflies.
Two orange-winged ones are flapping and gliding
in cracked loops beside the palms, and by my feet
two more with spotted ivory wings are dancing
or fighting or copulating – for what do I know
of the lives and drives, the intricate body parts,
of butterflies – before vanishing beyond the pond ...

Remembering rain is often about forgetting, absence,
the sweet melancholy it may induce. Sub-species,
I know, of a pathetic fallacy I can't resist.
Rain washes down the pink brick of St Josephs
Catholic Church and soaks the barely visible,
uncertain blossoms of early spring. Night's chill
approaches and the sun is a spilling milky-grey.
What did we talk about while sheltering
in that high-ceilinged hall, the stained glass
dark above us with their stations of the cross?
That morning a strange motel and the muffled
confusions between day and night, wakefulness
and the stickiness of sleep. From the next room
a sudden flush then hush then slam and
a car engine choking into life. Left behind
a smattering of rain against the window ...

Strapped to my chest Baby Lulu snuffles, gurgles,
swings her head from side to side and contentedly
falls asleep. High above a Seahawk cranks its wings
in what appears a monstrous effort to hold fast,
then, effortlessly, is still and poised, then plummets
to within feet of the sea before, without perceptible adjustment,
soaring up and away. Balanced on a light pole
a cormorant flaps his wings and hangs them out to dry.
A wind-driven cabbage moth makes its zig-zag
reconnaissance up and down, here and there,
its white frailty a speck against the blue enormity
of the sea where, far out, the spout and rolling back
of a whale returning south can just be glimpsed.
A small boy walking past tells his mum, 'If
you take the mass of the universe and convert it
all to energy …' then he's gone …

I'm walking across a barren field, parkland, I suppose.
It's not yet summer though a nor'westerly wind
swells with heat. Already the grass is brown, sparse,
and full of weeds, always weeds. Netball lights
tower to the left, and in the distance sprinklers twitch
and twirl and soak the football fields. Behind me
the Moscow Circus has erected tents whose minarets
slice up and mock the sky. Three teenage boys amble
towards the fields. One skips ahead, slips his T-shirt off,
then his shorts, then runs naked through the sprinklers.
Modestly, one hand remains clutched around his balls
while the other hand grips his shorts. Why?
It's obvious. Had he trusted the shorts to his friends
they would have dashed away. We would have,
when we were fifteen …

Everything waste
everything would be or was
C. K. Williams

The swollen belly of the basin stretches on forever and forever,

swells to the four compass points and pushes against far fringing banks which

in the fading light of dusk appear as silhouettes, black, irregular borders, impenetrable, enclosing.

A last light glitters off the surface, flicking the rills and ruffles a weak southerly has conjured up.

On the near shore mounds of seaweed dry and bleach and crackle

under our bare feet. At the water's edge livid green strands tangle and flop like snakes writhing in a B-grade horror movie.

A plover picks its way daintily through the mess, its quick beak darting back and forth, in and out, as the mass moves under it.

The unseen, underwater thrust and pull, the little heaving here and there, the wrenching up and

relocating, this reed to rubbish movement; air, water, light, each cell born and sub-dividing, growing

on its way to stiff, brittle wrack, to breaking down and stinking here on the shore under our bare feet

crunching and lumbering while we think about so much beauty
        and so much death,

and beauty in the process, the pre-determined,
        chancy, not-quite-random process.

The rough dark trees behind us are twisted and bent by time, by weather,
        by the sun sparkling off their leaves.

Here the fallen cones of banksia men, here the backbone of a fish, here the
        carcass of a bird,

the plover, unconcerned, intent, lifting those twig-like legs and
        positioning them so precisely,

our feet pressing down, pressing on, stumbling forward in our ungainly
        gait, eyes downcast,

uplifted. Is that a sail out towards the heads? Is it going out or slowly
        coming about

in a breeze the canvas barely holds? Where is anchorage for the sailor on
        the sea,

the cormorant now skimming the surface, the fish grazing on weed,
        flicking their tails, drifting by rock and shell?

What if we could hold all this like the sail almost holds the breeze,

hold the instant even for an instant before it lifts and wavers, lifts and falls,
        shuddering here

before drawing back and up again, the cell dividing, the weed decaying,
>   the plover

in his elegant gavotte, the fish and birds even now gliding from our sight,

stop it all from passing into memory, into yearning, forgetfulness,
>   slipping beyond the boundaries of the self?

Sometime soon, Phobos, nearest moon to Mars, will quaver,
>   crack, be split apart by gravity's relentless pull

and the mass of rubble will be gathered into spinning rings so
>   Mars resembles Saturn. It does not hold, it will be held.

I hold your hand, the soft pad which hides a trace of pulse, the
>   heart line, life line,

and faint blue hints of blood, the creases time has wrought and
>   can't undo, hold, touch, all that is passing on and through,

We turn and head for home, leave behind the bird, the fish, the sail,
>   glance back for one last look and see

a two-person pedal kayak trundle into view, its wake subsiding
>   as quickly as it's made. It's heading east, the sun is at
>   its stern,

in the back seat a woman, straight-backed, intent, holds a parasol
>   against the dying light.

Only keep still, wait, and hear
and the world will open
Richard Powers

Wind, cloud, waves, the seemingly erratic
flitterings of birds, sunrise and sunset, ever determined,
make room for the unexpected, the engaging.
Not quite anything can happen. Something is withheld,
missing or misplaced. Something is added. The ambiguous
comes to life, is life, is puzzlement, possibility.

I'm always writing about the sea, about change,
about power, how small we are, I am; about
being tossed around, lost maybe, in the grip
of something we can't theorise or subdue. Am I
most myself or not myself when I'm in the sea?
Have I pulled on another mask with my costume
and my fins? Can I be myself when I am
afraid, uncertain, boastful, thrilled? Proliferating 'me's
like the 'me's that are always me in anxious dreams,
re-working past events askew and altered, waking
to another me, the surface beneath the surface rising
to accommodate the known unknown world.

Here's my plan. To sit in one spot, perhaps on a balcony
looking through rainforest to the sea, from sunrise
to sunset and record everything I see. All that is not me.
The bigger than usual black ant that skirmishes
near my feet, the fern that's jittering in a bowl,
the shadow growing wider on the marbled floor, the gnats
and cabbage moths and dragonflies, an emerald-winged butterfly
swooping among the leaves, the visible invisible spider web,
moss figuring or disfiguring a stone wall, the leafless

frangipani, the blotched and mottled tree trunks,
epiphytes, scarlet bougainvillea bloom, palm trees,
strangler vines, a drab brown bird, wings flared,
feet outstretched, landing on a swaying branch
and disappearing in the foliage, and through the gaps
blue glimpses of the sea, the sound of falling waves
which may be big or small, the call, the screech,
the chirp, the bell and peck of birds, a far-off hammering,
a voice in a foreign-sounding tongue. All that
is outside me, distant, unambiguous but not certain,
not fixed or absolute. The wind is getting up now.
Branches sway, leaves flap and bob and fling about,
are flung about, and fall. And I'm an hour in
to an Arcadian anti-Warhol fantasy, me asserting
and selecting, an old chameleon whose colours flicker
with the light, fade disjointedly and settling, refuse to settle ...

Echo, repetition, statement
and counterstatement, digression and return
Robert Hass

Here's a second plan, another to unmask the world.
I'll sit at a footpath café in an up and coming part of town,
sip coffee, and record everything I see. The bumper-to-bumper
impatient flood of cars, the weaving two-wheeled bikes
and bicycles, pigeons pecking for a crumb, dawdling
or purposeful pedestrians, this one with a hat,
this one bareheaded, the businessman in his business suit,
the lady with a pram, the girl in thongs and a midriff top,
the tattooed, beanied boy bouncing his skateboard
up the gutter, that louche fellow dragging on a cigarette
and leaning mysteriously into a shadowed wall,
the madman waving his arms about and talking to himself
or maybe that's a mobile thingy jammed in his ear.
A street sweeper's orbital brushes pointlessly polish tar,
tires hiss, engine noise rises and falls above and below
a constant hum, a bus growls, a horn bleats,
cups and saucers and teaspoons clink, papers rustle and flap,
and snippets of conversation flutter at my ears. It's noisy.

I've just read a sign in a hairdresser's window:
'for a head worth mounting.' What does that mean?
What were they thinking? I guess that's ambiguity for you
or irony, but not the kind I'm thinking of. Perhaps it's sincerity,
or bad taste or just annoying, like bumper stickers –
teachers do it with class – or the hand therapist
I visited yesterday whose reception brochure promised vision,
mission, and to 'work hand-in-hand for a healthier you.'

I'm too noisy. Understanding lies in silence, in the rests
between the words, the spaces left for you to saunter
round and back before I'm at your ear again,
mumbling over the joint between chaos and some order,
worrying at self-made problems of fact and fiction,
the ludicrous confusions about what can be seen and known,
the something, nothing, everything logic of a Rubik's cube.

Mostly we read in silence, silence which might allow us
to throw off the masks or as many as we dare. Is the aim
to be inside or outside ourselves, where does the danger lie?
St. Augustine tells us Ambrose of Milan was the first man
to read without moving his lips. To Augustine
this was amazing, to us an unremarkable fact of life.
That's it, isn't it? The importance of time and place,
the pre-suppositions we can't escape no matter
how rational, objective, open-minded we think we are.
What leaves me puzzled, skating thought to thought,
appears to you pellucid. Multiple 'me's appear and disappear
dissolve and re-combine, rush forward snarling,
withdraw in fear, then form a queue from the smallest
to the largest. 'Choose which one,' they mock, 'the one
essential me' and start to fade. There must be more
than seven types of ambiguity, just think: the courtroom dust
a QC casts, the shapes a politician's promise can assume,
the silliness of trying to impose one reading on any text,
the certain uncertainties I have about the world …

The brown current
ran swiftly out of the heart of darkness
Joseph Conrad

Streetlights on the sea at night, pale yellow, white, stretching out,
    wavering
and bobbing with the current, the wind-sifted waves. The limits
    of illumination.
The mind's eye is not reliable, it sees and does not see, cannot
    solve the problem,
'how can I describe?', cannot solve the problem, 'how is it
    possible to explain?'

        Sixteen years into the Peloponnesian War
        with Sparta, Athens lay siege to the island
        of Melos which had remained neutral.
        The Athenians starved the inhabitants into
        surrender, put to death the adult males and
        enslaved the women and children.

Day moves on to day and days and Wedding Cake Island floats
    somewhere to the north
of Coogee Beach, floats seemingly to the south and then,
    surprisingly,

        During the Third Punic War, Roman legions
        besieged Carthage, storming the walls in
        146BC and slaughtering the defenders on
        a scale unprecedented in history. That the
        land was sown with salt is a nineteenth
        century elaboration.

is anchored in Lurline Bay. Behind the beach once was swamp,
    peat, and rush-like sedge.

In spring and summer Fan-tailed Warblers called from the top of
    Typha reeds.

> In the thirteenth century the armies of Ghengis Khan swept into Central Asia and Eastern Europe destroying whole towns, farmland, livestock, domestic animals and entire populations. One million people were killed at the sacking of Urgench. Ghengis Khan styled himself the 'flail of god.'

and Bracelet Honey-myrtle, bent flat, all twisted by on-shore,
    salt-steeped winds.
The whales are heading north this morning, three spouts half-
    way to the horizon

> Conflict between white settlers and Native Americans lasted from colonial times until 1890. More than forty declared Indian wars which cost the lives of 19,000 whites and 30,000 Indians are recorded. Surviving Indians were forced onto reservations. This was Manifest Destiny.

off Bronte Beach. Scant months from now they'll be heading
    south again,
calves swimming at their flanks. I think I've swum with whales, a
    whale.

> During Australia's frontier wars spears lost out to single-shot breech-loading rifles, the Martini-Henry and the Winchester time and time again. More than 20,000 Aboriginals may have perished though pedants insist this number is a fabrication.

I think I saw a spout not once but twice not fifty metres from
    where I floated
well within the exclusion zone. Winter's sharp, bright blue sea
    slots fast into the cliffs,

> For twenty-three years from 1895 King
> Leopold II of Belgium burned villages
> in the Congo, kidnapped children, cut off
> heads, hands and genitals, flogged and
> starved the population to encourage them
> to extract rubber. Ten million died. Leopold
> never set foot in the Congo.

into every cleft and cranny, every cave and crevice, every vent and
    crack
as though a master craftsman had finished off the dovetailing
    and pronounced it good.

> After wars in Ireland, Scotland, Europe, Asia
> and Australasia, India, Africa and North
> America, Britain controlled lands on which
> the sun never set. It exported opium to
> China and slaves to the Caribbean. During
> the Boer War it invented the concentration
> camp. No one has calculated how many died
> in pursuit of empire.

Yesterday a surfer drowned caught beween rocks called 'The
    Twins' and pounded
by a rising swell, his head cracked against the cliff and his body
    washed ashore.

> From 1915 the Ottomon Empire
> systematically slaughtered Armenian men
> and drove the women and children into the

259

desert where they were beaten, robbed, raped, starved and murdered. As many as one and a half million perished. The word 'genocide' was coined to describe the massacre. Officially it never happened.

Rescuers worked furiously to revive him on the freezing, gritty sand. Tamarama
is a dangerous beach, cliffs on either side, rips on either side, steep, narrow,

> Joseph Stalin's policy of collectivization turned the entire Ukraine into a concentration camp by 1933 and induced a famine known as 'Holodomor.' 25,000 people starved or were shot each day and in all seven million Ukrainians may have lost their lives.

one spot becomes a mixing bowl in heavy surf. In 1906 an entrepreneur
built Wonderland City here. It was, they said, the Coney Island of the south

> In December 1937 Japanese troops captured Nanjing and in the weeks that followed 30,000 civilians and disarmed combatants were bayoneted, decapitated, machine-gunned, and buried alive. Women were gang-raped, babies were cut from the womb. Ultra-nationalists deny or minimize the atrocities.

and boasted an Airem Scarem which swung cliff to cliff when it hadn't broken down
leaving revellers strung above the surf. Unloved by locals it closed in 1911.

In 1940 the Germans bombed London and
fifteen other British cities. This was known
as the Blitz and forty thousand died. In
retaliation the Allies flew 363 air raids over
Berlin (50,000 killed), firebombed Hamburg
(40,000 killed) and Dresden (Operation
Gomorrah: 25,000 killed), bombed Kassel,
Darmstadt, Pforzheim... This was termed
Total War.

At North Bondi Aboriginal carvings of a whale, fish, mundoes
and humans
can be seen in sandstone behind the cliffs near the sewage works
ventilation shaft.

The Holocaust (Shoah) is so well-known.
Under Hitler the Nazis exterminated six
million European Jews. First there was
a theory, then propaganda, then laws
and yellow stars, persecution, expulsion,
concentration camps, ghettos, cattle
trucks and gas chambers. They also
killed Communists, Gypsies, blacks and
homosexuals. Neo-Nazis do exist. The
Holocaust has been denied.

Others may be hidden under golf course turf. 'Mundoes depict
the pathway
to adulthood. Little remains of the area's harsh, pre-European
landscape.

One night in 1945 B-29 Superfortresses
dropped incendiary bombs on Tokyo. One
hundred thousand burned to death. Raids
followed on Kobe, Osaka, and Nagoya. An
atomic bomb (Little Boy) was dropped

261

on Hiroshima on 6 August and three days later another (Fat Boy) on Nagasaki. Up to 100,000 may have died immediately from the blast and many more slowly from radiation sickness.

of heath, low woodland, coast rosemary and banksia scrub.
When I was growing up
the land behind Maroubra Beach was sand dunes, slippery, shifting and untidy.

When British India was partitioned in 1947 half a million died in communal violence. Fourteen million Hindus, Muslims and Sikhs were displaced. In 1971, in the consequential war in Bangladesh, up to three million may have been killed. More than 200,000 women were tortured, raped and kept as sex slaves. This was called Operation Searchlight. Tensions between India and Pakistan persist.

Gradually housing estates wound round the hills, gutters, paths and lawns
divided up the space; and blocks of flats began the silent struggle against corrosion.

Mao Zedong initiated the Great Leap Forward in 1958. Anywhere between eighteen and thirty million Chinese died of malnutrition or were directly killed. In 1966 he launched the Cultural Revolution. Millions more were forcibly relocated, publicly humiliated, imprisoned, tortured and murdered by Red Guards.

A riding school and rifle range still dominate the southern
    headland and signs warn us
to 'Beware', 'Keep Out'. The weather gives no hint that this
    is winter.

> Pol Pot declared 1975 Year Zero in Democratic Kampuchea and embarked on a Super Great Leap Forward. Twenty five percent of the population died from starvation, overwork, torture and execution. A network of mass graves became known as The Killing Fields.

The sea is almost summer warm, the sun is gentle in a baby-
    blanket sky and people
stroll the promenade pushing prams. The immeasurable,
    the unanswerable,

> The disintegration of Yugoslavia led to years of Balkan conflict. The town of Sarajevo was bombarded for fourteen hundred days by artillery, rockets, mortars and machine gun fire. Snipers were especially feared. 10,000 died. Despite being a UN declared 'safe area' 6,000 Bosnian men were slaughtered when Srebrenica was overrun in 1995. War crimes tribunals are proceeding.

keeps breaking in, is rationalized, forgotten, consigned to
    another time and place.
How does one think proportion, how retain memory in a
    changing world

> In one hundred days in mid-1994 almost one million Rwandans were massacred with machetes, clubs and rifles when the Hutu

> majority attacked the Tutsi minority. Rape and vaginal mutilation were weapons. HIV infection was deliberate. The international community was slow to act.

which doesn't change? Always a stretch of cliff is different. The
    future is adrift,
the past a wreck, and maps will never be a substitute for time
    and place.

> On September 11 2001 al-Qaeda crashed two planes into the Twin Towers of the World Trade Centre in New York. Smoke and debris engulfed the area, 3,000 died. In reprisal America invaded Afghanistan and Iraq. Over 170,000 civilians died before the Americans began a staged withdrawal. We may soon be back.

The moon's one face gives way to many faces, many moons
circle round the earth, circle round unseen, elliptically
the earth goes round a dying star, all things gripped and held
just so, braced not to fly apart or hurtle into one another ...

A preposterous hodgepodge
uniquely arranged
Inga Clendinnen

It's too hard to imagine the future or understand
the past. We make best guesses, reassure
or deceive ourselves, add or subtract
from day to day. Even the present is
more or less confusing. I am dancing

to the off-key music unravelling in my head
and my steps are awkward, stumbling, because my ears
resist the beat. All around me dancers twirl,
dip and pirouette, two-step, tango, twist
in frantic time as a gypsy band plays louder,

faster, and more erratically. In the centre of the floor
Felix Dzerzhinsky goes on his knees to Anna Akhmatova
and Ezra Pound clasps Joseph Brodsky to his chest; T.S. Eliot
waltzes Mao Zedong around the room while,
over in a corner, Joseph Stalin sobs to Shostakovich,

'I've been misunderstood.' And who's that arm in arm?
Why it's Kennedy and Khrushchev watching fascinated
William Wordsworth stepping out a fierce fandango all alone.
Champagne fountains burble, flames leap and a Black Widow
shows Snow White her dance card full of names.

My broken dance becomes a voice, limping just behind
or just below the music, in its crazed and bleeding tones
a history of wind, of rain, of birds, of the day
after day, sun behind clouds, mist between trees,
seaweed rocking back and forth. Dietrich Bonhoeffer

peeps between the curtains. Bodies dangle at the end of ropes,
heads topple into baskets, tongues cry out as sand
engulfs their mouths. Churchill drops his poison gas
on Lenin's troops, Mandelstam waits for clothes
which don't arrive. Mayakovsky puts a bullet in his brain.

Speak, sing, dance. Only listen. To the ravens
and the doves, seagulls, swifts, the tiny wren,
the albatross and eagle, the mutton birds –
shearwaters – on their perilous journeys
season after season to breed or flop into the sea.

Awake in the dark of 5am in a strange bed
in an unmoored city with that drifting
space-module feeling motel rooms may induce.
And then I hear it. The double-down, rippling
magpie call from home. Distant, definite,

now three notes, now two. Is that
an answering call, a link? And then it stops.
Silence but for the slight, sinister, other-worldly rattle
of the air conditioner – as if air
should be conditioned. And now as the module

races on to Mars, the red and rocky planet,
mad hope of space survivalists, the band once more
picks up the bagpipes, drums, fiddles,
trumpets, bells, clappers, hand grenades. That music,
could it be the music of the spheres ...

What were they then
that are what they are now
A.R. Ammons

A baby-boomer who dodged the war in Vietnam, who didn't
have the gumption to conscientiously object, who marched
anonymously in all the demonstrations but somehow
couldn't bring himself to chant 'Ho, Ho, Ho Chi Minh,'
I taught history for twenty years and could argue
the distinctions to be drawn between Vladimir Ilyich Ulyanov
and Joseph Stalin, the reasons Weimar failed and Hitler
overreached himself, how Mao Zedong outmanoeuvred
the Guomindang, why India had to be divided. I had
a cynical, pacifist, left-wing handle on what it was
made this world tick. But on Anzac Day I struggle not to cry.
Not at the speeches of the politicians, the parades,
the theme park Gallipoli has become, but at the playing
of the Last Post and for the photographs of those boys,
those chiselled handsome men who did not come back
or now are ninety, ninety-five, one hundred, and look
just like my grandfather, like my father may have looked,
who have settled into wrinkles, canes, dementia and who
we can't believe we will ever be or ever could become …

The lightness, the non-mass of it
how the scales of the real world hardly registered it
Niall Williams

Water-laden, the air is falling. The immediate future
is indistinct. Palm trees lose their certainty,
droop and merge, loom and disappear. Unearthliness
of earth. Does land float, sea swim?
Are the birds still wheeling? Do they
shelve beaks beneath wings or, unwilling
to be caught off guard, swivel their heads
side to side? The sun will burn it off, I know,
the wind blow it clear. The bay's wide open mouth
will empty and the sky blaze blue once more but,
for the moment, my body takes on aspects of this grey ...

A flock-edged strip of light leaps off the sea. Nothing
is now visible. To swim out our take off on a wave
is an act of faith or hope or, more modestly,
an act of recklessness or frustration, a refusal
to forgo the wave no matter what potential hazard
might lie beneath its drop: rocks, an abandoned board, another
similarly afflicted surfer taking his own chances ...

I float on my belly as still as can be
in the softly lulling swell. Sea-grasses
and rasp-edged kelp float back and forth in unison
or a quarter tone off key, caught and tweaked
by competing currents. Splotched and striped fish,

some no bigger than my fingernail, play catch as catch can
among the foliage. They dart and twist, scribble and flicker
as bigger fish glide by unperturbed. The blue groper
snuffles on the seabed, digs in, flicks up sea urchins
in a veil of sand. Sun filters down and lingers,
sifts and shifts what was once unseen ...

Pools, puddles, ponds, rivers, lakes, the sea,
reflect the sky. Clouds flex their muscles here
then slip away, drift beneath the sun and manifest
as the weightless weight we assign to them. Premonition
we can't pin down. Tense and time change everything,
memory masquerades as a dream or nightmare
or the shaped confusion in between: a landscape
we grub for understanding. Rain spits,
pocks sea's secret skin, shatters the illusion ...

Last night's rain is strung on early morning grass,
globes of light glisten and it looks
as if it might crackle underfoot and then
it looks soft and yielding, the green stems
bowed under transparent weight.
'Crystalline' could be the word. But no, that's a
false impression. 'Hazed'? A silky gleam
clings to the leaves, mist rises through reeds
and a knuckled light leaches from the clouds,
contends with rain, gives us rain,
It passes through me or I through it,
it locks on to the receptors of my eyes,
the air I breathe, the boundary that I tread ...

❦

It's the something which is nothing that I like,
the immaterial that is embodied, that comes and goes
in particles or waves, makes for the ground, is grounded,
is in the world, is there but not there at a speed we calculate
but barely apprehend in shades and shadows, pits and chasms,
pinpricks, shafts, blooms, blotches, freckles, blisters on my skin;
that slices through the sky without volition or desire, a revelation
that shineth but doesn't draw attention to itself, yet attends,
becomes flesh that is not flesh, that glints and winks
and strokes my back when my back is turned, warms
the cockles of my heart, blows the blues away, that doesn't know
but knows; invisibility which makes it possible to see …

❦

Even here it's the verbal that intrudes,
words stretching for a sticking place or lips
straining for a word commensurate
and coming up short, our point of difference
letting us down or cutting us loose in a picturesque
we colour by numbers and gradually believe.
How many lies do we tell ourselves, how often
do we deceive? *Something, maybe the soul,*
Chase Twichell writes, *says language is a whip
that hurts it.* She's right, I think, and
though my compass tells me north from south
I don't know where to go from here, two dimensions
which only hint at three, a half-life lived by halves.
I write the same poem over and over again, never
getting it right, never breaking through
into that clear light, that lightness – the whip
twitching at my back, if not my soul …

Clinging to my shoulder like a soft faced cockatoo,
Lulu points to the western sky and in her two-year-old tongue
gabbles, "Moon, moon, moon." I ask Buster, her almost
five-year-old brother, if it's full. 'I don't think so,'
he answers seriously, 'it's a little bit lopsided.'
Behind us ripples of sunrise splash against retreating cloud,
'Moon, moon,' Lulu insists, patting my bald head ...

There on the shore
of the wide world I stand
John Keats

Not quite four years old, Mr Keaton
stands on the quarterdeck of the caravel
his father has built for him. Close-rigged,
slung from the ceiling by ropes of steel,
it sways above the lounge room floor where,
amongst the sea-wrack of toys and baby bottles,
his twin sisters loll and roll like mermaids
or squalling, unassuming sirens. He grips the rails.
Around him his crew of super-heroes – Hulk,
Batman, the Flash – go about their duties
keeping his world free from whatever evil
a young mind might summon up. Seven seas
and seven peaks await him, sunsets and stars
unnumbered, spice isles, sandy beaches, tempests
and leeward shoals; strange lands where anthropophagi
flit between the trees. The wind gets up a sliver,
instant upon instant lying head to tail
in the time it takes him to trim the sails.
Keaton turns from the far horizon, ties down the wheel,
for now he plans to anchor securely here at home.

A steady delete
of anything that tells us what we are
John Burnside

Walking the mile or so to school through suburban
1950s streets, a rag-tag gang of boys and girls

swelling as we progressed, we'd bark at dogs,
trip each other up, steal a shoe and throw it

up a tree, run away to see which stragglers
would be left behind. Trailing once the bigger boys,

I heard a shout of 'Look out, shit!', saw the pack divide,
but didn't know where the danger lay, which way to run,

where this shit was hiding, or what it might do
if I fell into its hands. At a later date I blushed

when I learnt the meaning of the word. In Transition,
Miss Purvis kept me in one recess because I'd dared

to add loops to a line of 'r's in running writing class.
At lunchtime I knocked myself unconscious

chasing Gregory Goldsmith when he swerved and I crashed
into the brick wall of the school. I took turns with Angela

and Linda to come first in class and don't know why
it mattered, or why I'm embarrassed to be telling this to you ...

Drive, he sd
for Christ's sake, look / out where yr going
Robert Creeley

It's 1968 again, the year that's squashed between
a summer of love and landing on the moon.

My hair is brushed and precisely ruffled so it's
a tangled sway three-finger's width below my years.

The Nehru collar on the op shop shirt,
frayed jeans and a denim jacket

are enough to signify. Or betray. Who
is this figure trying to be? Or trying

not to be. It's the year of the Tet offensive,
when Norman Mailer wrote *Armies of the Night*

and Martin Luther King was killed, when the Beatles
recorded 'Hey Jude' and 'Lady Madonna' and my first car,

a green, clapped-out Morris Isis, was abandoned
by the gutter in Cleveland Street, and I

roamed the campus and the surf club in duplicate
or triplicate not being what I wanted, a stranger

even to myself. Were it possible to decide,
what would we keep of this not-quite-finished prodigal,

this anonymity pretending he's the one who's left the fold,
who knows he's running with the herd? ...

I should be rolling down the skyway
on my cosmic wheels
Donovan Leitch

This is a poem for anyone who wore flared jeans
with embroidered flowers around the cuffs,
who wore Jesus sandals and Hindu bracelets,
who, born in the heady aftermath of World War Two,
sang 'We Shall Overcome' secretly and softly
in their bedrooms at night and dreamed
of becoming Bob Dylan or a minor troubadour,
who read Mao and Marcuse and Carlos Castenada,
Genet and Gertrude Stein and Sartre and *Teaching
as a Subversive Activity*, who thought the sexual revolution
was a good idea and would have liked an invitation,
who grew Zapata moustaches and sat on their knees
chewing in macrobiotic restaurants, who went to India
to find themselves and ended up washing glasses
in a London pub as the swinging sixties waned.
Ginsberg on the finger cymbals, Beatles in the Himalayas,
Hippies turning into Yippies turning on to Kool-Aid
turning into Weathermen, stepping out with Charles Reich
accumulating orgones. Oh Donovan, your Hurdy Gurdy Man,
your Atlantis, Your Mellow Yellow Cosmic Wheels,
how did we survive you more-or-less intact ...

Stately, plump Buck Milligan
came from the stairhead bearing a bowl of lather
James Joyce

I've read Ulysses twice, thrice, yet remember
only snot green sea, that Mr Leopold Bloom 'ate with relish'
and, of course, the echo of Molly's dreamily ecstatic
'yes, yes, yes.' I've lost a leg with Ahab, been wounded
crouched next to Orwell on the Catalonian barricades,
gone three rounds with Papa Hemingway, Paris '29.
I've posted Herzog's unsent letters and felt a little icky
at the fascination which swept Humbert Humbert's life away.
Arm in arm with Tolstoy I stumbled after Counts and Countesses
and their spiralling-syllabled names, but still arrived a page too late
to snatch Anna from the tracks. I went within a whisker
of wriggling between *Catch 22*'s wickedly closing jaws.
God forgive me, I failed to reach the gates of *Paradise Regained*
and, while on confession, I scoffed the fabled madeleine
before I went to bed, then wallowed in the wordy bog
adjacent to *Swann's Way*. I've worn out many a pocket
swapping stones with Molloy, Murphy or Malone, inevitably
I mix them up. I need an intervention. I need a biblio-
psycho-therapist who might free me from the thrall
of all my readings past, the whimsy of living page by page.
My wife claims I spend my days trudging Roman Britain
looking for *The Eagle of the Ninth*, gorging on forbidden tuck
with Billy Bunter, the Owl of the Remove, or sailing
on Lake Windemere sometimes imagining I'm a Swallow,
or pretending I'm an Amazon. Sadly, all of the above is true ...

You want ghosts
and the daily news and prophecy
Robert Adams

It's been an ordinary life, so much like
so many others, not too many glories, not too many shames,
a mite's illumination. Perhaps a B+ life,

though that is dangerously close to boasting,
Each morning now I clamber to the beach
through a clifftop cemetery and sometimes

this coincides with sunrise and it's impossible
not to revel in the everyday banality. On Wednesday
a huge black cloud, jutting from the horizon

like a ragged mountain peak, blotted out the sun
but its rim, signifying the particularities of atmosphere,
was fringed by a silver, branching light. By Thursday

The coastline of a dark unknown continent hovered
in the mountain's place, the sky was ultramarine and bright,
and clouds were pink and orange vapour trails

or fairy floss. *Rosy fingered dawn* I suppose,
though that's almost too figured to comprehend.
Dawn is in the body without need of epithets.

Here I am re-jigging things in Wonderland.
I imagine other presents, tidy up the past,
sketch out glittering futures, if not glittering

at least brighter, a little striking. I like it here.
In Wonderland there are mysteries and there are puzzlements
which I have no need to solve, 'known unknowns

and unknown unknowns' to quote a swine
who knew a thing or too. In Wonderland or the cemetery
I've never seen a ghost. I never expect to

though I've been startled by a sudden scrabbling
when it's dark or felt thought slide when clouds unexpectedly
deny the light. Ghosts are the stuff of stories, a disposition

to look outside the self for answers or consolation.
All things glow and fade though the gravestones all
are fixed, the angels mute, the cemetery …

is real estate. Shadows are the nearest thing
to ghosts. You can't call shadows substance
but you can sense their arrival and departure, their creeping,

that their imprint is proof of substance, the disclosed
and undisclosed in abeyance. Shadows are an intercession
between me and not me, a suspension

between 'I feel' and 'it must mean.' Words
shadow other words, shadow other worlds. They are ghosts,
they are clouds. I know them by their fuzzy edges.

❦

The old verities – Christianity, Communism, rhyme and metre –
are dimmed and dogma masquerades
as something else – economics maybe. Theory.

All poetry's didactic, at least to some extent,
and it's all descriptive, narrative and confessional,
to some extent. Words line up, drop down a line,

line up again, and you stand behind each word you write
no matter how you try to hide, no matter
the stratagems you employ. You choose to choose

to roll a die, pluck marbles from a sack, mash together
the daily paper and an obscure evangelical tract
but even if meaning is meaningless to you,

your reader will bring meaning to the work
or try to. Words are clues, hints. I am groping
to say a thing which vanishes in the utterance.

This morning the rain-splashed, glass-grey dimpling
of the sea is unvaried, seems unvaried,
though gutters, sandbanks and channels, the ebbing tide

all leave hints of movement, change, unmeasured depth.
I see little more than surface, marvel
when schools of salmon leap or cormorants dive,

give only passing thought to the Continental Shelf, to ground swell,
the East Australian Current, all the other forces
at play below my gaze. These too are layerings of time,

the long time of cooling and warming seas, the seasonal shifts
of winds and currents, the uncertain arrivals
of la Niña and el Niño, the daily tracked and timed

alterations of the tide. There is a patience in this predictability
and unpredictability, a waiting and a willingness
to speculate. From this angle or that perspective, day after day,

in painting after painting, an artist friend tries to capture light,
not capture, not even render, tries to apprehend light's temptations
on cloud and sea. It's a search for the invisible in what is visible,

something that depends on sense but is beyond the senses,
what cannot be expressed without distortion: the reflective
and absorbent qualities of water, the way it is sometimes grey,

sometimes blue or green, sometimes so reflective it is invisible
and simultaneously opaque: the texture of this world in time and place.
It strikes me this is ground on which to stand ...

A spring day like this
how yellow the air is
Carol Frost

And here's the elephant in the room: beauty
and all that trails after it, all that is
imbedded in it: a waxing moon, a waning moon,
the mountain, chasm, mudflat, wetland, the river
slithering down and through a valley full of trees,
cliffs and crags and mangrove swamps; and my favourites,
the fierce beauty of a breaking wave, the brilliance
of the sun coming up even more than the sun going down;
the colour burst of spring, the purple jacaranda, a yellow
winter wattle bloom ...

                    flowers picked this morning and arranged
in a vase, ornamental carp – red, silver, gold –
circling beneath a bridge, the skill that turns a colour field –
a heap of steel, a carved stone – into something different,
made, the mysteries of music tapping at the ear, the sentence
that takes your breath away ...

                    that fades but doesn't pall;
a tree ecstatic with the raucous flutter of birds,
a bank of darkening cloud swelling to the south,
the sudden pelt of rain; Venus, Helen, Adonis, James Dean,
a tiger stalking through bamboo, Muybridge's horse;
fire, inferno, Christ on the cross; what, unknowingly,
we are trained to see, which flouts the rules,
which is reason's resting place; the eye of Hokusai
getting better as he aged ...

                beauty that blinds,
that is in the eye, the act of seeing which makes a moment
substance which can be shared, which can't
be shared, not really, though words may be passed around;
beauty which is a puzzle, but no secret, which prevails
despite our claims; moments which come and go
and come again, that are more than momentary,
more than a distraction …

                from the ugliness that abounds,
beauty which looks back at us, tells us who we are,
the fitness of this goes with that which might explain the world
but can't; concord teetering on the edge of discord,
pleasure not always unalloyed, compromised by words
like 'nature', 'culture', 'spirit', 'soul', by an unwillingness
to let go. That ' the most beautiful is the most just'
is Delphic and untrue …

                but still. Long after my father-in-law
lost his speech to Alzheimer's, when we were crossing
Sydney Harbour in early evening light,
out of the blue he spoke one word: 'beautiful' …

Endless forms most beautiful and wonderful
have been and are being evolved
Charles Darwin

There must be evidence, proof, a theory,
these hands, these eyes, the mind's eye settling
and moving on, restless as the apple

before it hits the ground which never
hits the ground, never leaves the branch
though it bobs and sways in a light-fingered wind.

Newton drowsing in early autumn warmth,
thinking Leibnitz, dreaming thoughts alchemical,
evolution taking place *whenever and wherever*

opportunity offers as invisibly as his laws of motion,
but too slow to see except when looking backwards.
Newton theorized a peacock's iridescence and,

presumably without his knowledge, animals adapt
so one hundred eye spots on the peacock's feathers seem
two hundred when he shakes them, and the peahen

is suitably impressed. So beetles change their shape
to reduce their shadows, butterflies look bigger
than they are, and jellyfish roll to appear transparent.

It all depends on light, the angle from which you're looking…

※

Every day I see the sea, the way it laps up
or slaps and lingeringly falls back, reliably
or violently running in and out. A southerly wind

may bring surf or make a mess
of any waves there were, a strong nor-easter
could drop the temperature a degree or two.

This month I've seen a shark-fin rock
slice through the sand and gradually
submerge again. The other day the beach

was full of weed and on the tideline
among the feathers, leaves, driftwood, pumice,
shells, dead mutton birds fallen

exhausted from the sky, and fleets of bluebottles
stretched and stranded, drying in the sun,
were clumps of aluminium cans, corroded,

dented, bleached as though they had been bobbing
somewhere out to sea for months or years, an unlikely
ugly raft. It was Herbert Spencer

who first coined the term 'survival of the fittest' …

※

Pangea creaks, shifts, splits, drifts and acquires
that now familiar shape, the refinement
and rubbing away, the slow accretion

and sudden violent change. Single cells and everything
the same for an eternity of years. And then
biology's Big Bang when animals got eyes and shells,

teeth and tentacles, scales and claws. We are made of starlight,
carbon, we lived in hot volcanic pools, we stepped out of the sea,
a swimming worm the first of the phylum to which we belong.

The Reef's alive and corals, anemones, jellyfish are cousins.
In the Northern Territory they've discovered one hundred
previously unknown snails who've secretly been keeping up

with all that's changed over countless years. We drill cores deep
into Antarctic ice to look for time, for evidence of what might have been
and therefore what might be yet to come.

It's the cliché that is true: change the only constant ...

Growing up for me was carefree as many
of my age recall it. Not entirely –
I had the usual doubts, embarrassments,

self-consciousness – but carefree in the sense
we weren't responsible and any little blips
were soon forgotten. Even Sunday morning

kneeling awkwardly in Stamina shorts – all I remember
is 'Rock of Ages' – was only an interruption
before the beach and salt-streaked, sunburned bodies

and surf-o-planes and lying to each other
about how big that last wave was.
When the wind and current were in the right

or wrong direction, the stinkpipe smell was overpowering
and we'd swim with things that don't bear mention.
No faecal counts, no warnings against bathing, sun exposure.

Now ocean outfalls are kilometres out to sea
and out of mind and nothing much — so we're told —
survives the tertiary stage of treatment. Every now and then

there is a whiff and one can sniff the careless past …

Slow, swollen swells driven north and stiffening,
shape up, form steep wedges edging even higher,
all angles, ledges, slabs, sections about to fall,

and the rational mind plays tricks, the fragile body
shivers, freezes as excitement seems suddenly
fighting for one's life. The body swirls and tumbles,

is gripped, dragged down, down and even deeper,
stars flash and flicker and you fight an urge
to open wide your mouth. You're squashed to half your size,

then stretched elasto-man, your pointy skull
and elongated toes making for the sand,
the sky. From nowhere background scenery swells

and a tiny you is torn by birds and tangled up
in vines. Absurdly you find yourself remembering
the line of kings the witches showed Macbeth

and the terrible conclusions fear and guilt induced.
Once Hutcho caught a wave so big
he crossed Bronte Beach south to north

and surged straight up the stormwater channel
emerging minutes later in his Speedos
from a drain in Birrell Street. True story.

Well, maybe not. But this sort of thing makes me laugh …

Dogs in space, spiders, monkeys, men,
mice in labs and labyrinths running tests
against the clock, growing lethargic, anxious, ill,

4D printers as post-postmodern birth canals,
titanium, implants, plastic, stem cells, machines
which think and write themselves new futures,

Goldilocks skipping and capering at a new horizon,
singularity flaunting unimagined shapes and forms,
scoffing at Gödel as he mutters, 'No, no, impossible,'

long-line fishermen and factory trawlers
harvesting seas that warm and rise. In China
they're mining white asbestos after all we know.

The bloodshot eye of the sun leers unblinking
through smog and ash. The 'I' runs wild
How long before the fragments reach me here?

How long before the next Big Bang? Yet
after catastrophic fires this spring, cicadas
emerge from the subterranean years louder

and more numerous than we remember. How long
have they been on earth, how have they survived
since we collected them in boxes — a black prince

worth at least a dozen floury bakers …

೮

I planted a cycad seed because the packet
said it was the food of dinosaurs. I may have
planted it upside down. It was a joke

but something in me wanted this slight connection
to that far past to look at 'now'
and think 'ago'. Right now,

I'm sitting in a rooftop carpark
above a monstrous shopping mall.
Rain is pouring down and gusts of wind threaten

to overturn the car. Through racing cloud
and belching refinery smoke, yellow cranes materialize
like robotic warriors in an apocalyptic film.

They loom there on the skyline,
spindly metal legs threatening to stomp unthinkingly
over all that's ever been. Is this more fanciful

than to think the earth is fighting back ...

Broken/Beautiful

Schools of fish slide under me, a stingray
flicks up a mist of sand, a cormorant
breaks the surface, shakes his head and,

at the last second, all insouciance, slips under
the next breaking wave. I do too. Laboriously.
Seagulls speed past so low I fear my head's their target.

I've surfed with dolphins or they with me. It's not
unusual. Sometimes they're only two arm spans
to the side, so close you can see not only

the water-shedding, speeding shape but barnacles,
sores, chipped and broken fins, and though beautiful
it's unnerving when that much mammal

bursts from a wave. We know they talk to one another
but I swear they're laughing at our expense,
so slow, so cumbersome, so vulnerable we appear.

The music of time whips up the waves, whooses
through canyons and corridors, through the shivering limbs
of trees. A strong wind, a fluky wind, it stalls,

trips onward in the space between 'should'
and 'is', makes of this present
a non-negotiable past, or rather a past

the future will fuss over, pick apart and
re-assign. We hanker after knowing
and are given change, the predictable, unpredictable

pattern of the genes, of culture, of the naked body
clambering from the sea and stumbling, flippered,
four-footed on the sand. 'Our love affair with the world

begins with a broken heart.' I hear this out of context
from a Unitarian minister. Is it true or just fine-sounding,
self-romanticising? Would you believe me if I told you

the world is beautiful and we will break its heart?

www.ingramcontent.com/pod-product-compliance
Lightning Source LLC
Chambersburg PA
CBHW021144160426
43194CB00007B/687